WHEN THE HURT
RUNS DEEP

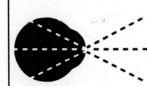

This Large Print Book carries the
Seal of Approval of N.A.V.H.

WHEN THE HURT RUNS DEEP

HEALING AND HOPE FOR LIFE'S DESPERATE MOMENTS

KAY ARTHUR

CHRISTIAN LARGE PRINT
A part of Gale, Cengage Learning

GALE
CENGAGE Learning·

Detroit • New York • San Francisco • New Haven, Conn • Waterville, Maine • London

GALE
CENGAGE Learning·

LIBRARY OF CONGRESS CATALOGING-IN-PUBLICATION DATA

Arthur, Kay, 1933–
   When the hurt runs deep : healing and hope for life's desperate moments / by Kay Arthur. — Large print ed.
      p. cm. — (Christian large print originals)
   Includes bibliographical references.
   ISBN-13: 978-1-59415-399-0 (softcover)
   ISBN-10: 1-59415-399-X (softcover)
   1. Consolation. 2. Suffering—Religious aspects—Christianity. 3. Large type books. I. Title.
   BV4905.3.A795 2011
   248.8'6—dc23   2011034321

Published in 2012 by arrangement with WaterBrook Press, an imprint of Crown Publishing Group, a division of Random House, Inc.

Printed in the United States of America
   1 2 3 4 5   15 14 13 12 11

FD349

*To my dear Billie and Gene Campbell,
who for almost forty years have lived out
the precepts of God as set forth in this
book, demonstrating for me His power,
which is perfected in our weaknesses. As
I have told you for years, Billie, there is a
place in my heart that is yours alone.*

*To the children and grandchildren of my
precious and courageous "Deborah,"
Nancy Schaefer. May you live not in the
light of the temporal tragedy of your
grandmother's death, but in the example
of her righteous, unflinching courage in
the midst of a corrupt and perverse
generation. Never forget she served as a
Deborah in the times when everyone did
what was right in their own eyes.*

*To all my Facebook friends who shared
your stories with me that I might better
minister the sufficiency of His grace and*

*the peace that passes all understanding
when you know that you know
God is sovereign.*

*To Krista and Art, who so generously
loaned us your summer home so I could
write this book on my favorite lake,
surrounded by the beauty of His creation
and loving friends. We felt cared for,
refreshed, restored . . . and loved with
His love through you. Thank you, dear
ones, for ministering to us in this
selfless way.*

CONTENTS

CHAPTER ONE:
"IT WASN'T SUPPOSED TO BE THIS WAY!"

At some point in life, nearly every one of us finds ourselves pulled under by a tsunami wave of pain, overwhelmed by something large, sudden, and personally devastating.

It can come crashing into our lives in any of a thousand ways.

A phone call from the doctor about a lab report that looks suspicious.

A wooden-faced supervisor who calls you into his office just before lunch and says, "We're downsizing the company. We have to let you go."

A brief, cold conversation with your spouse one morning, and then the shocking words: "I'm leaving. I've found someone else."

A late-night knock on your door from a highway-patrol officer. "Your daughter has been in an accident. I'm sorry to tell you this, but she didn't make it."

A quick, stricken glance from the obstetrician. "I'm not picking up any heartbeat from the baby."

At such times heartache and despair rush over us, pulling us down into a place of darkness until we wonder if the light of hope will ever again penetrate our lives.

This is when the hurt runs deep.

As human beings, hurts and wounds, bumps and bruises, disappointments and sorrows come bundled along with our birth certificates.

Every one of us, starting in childhood, had to learn how to deal with the skinned knees, hurt feelings, dashed hopes, and heartbreaking setbacks common to fallen humanity. How well we coped with these difficulties, challenges, and unexpected obstacles determined in large measure what sort of man or woman we've become and how we navigate our way through life.

But there are storms . . . and there are storms.

It's one thing to get caught in a spring thundershower; it's another to find yourself in a Category 5 hurricane. It's one thing to trip over a hose and fall in your backyard; it's another to fall out of a third-story window. It's one thing to be rejected for admission to college; it's another to be betrayed and rejected by the one you love with all your heart. It's one thing to lose your car keys; it's another to lose a longed-for baby in a miscarriage. It's one thing to get knocked off your feet by a surprise ocean wave, when you're looking in the other direction; it's another to be swallowed by a tsunami of pain.

Sometimes the pain we experience goes much, much deeper than surface pain. Sometimes the heartache we have to endure pierces deeper than we ever thought possible, utterly overwhelming us.

In my own life . . .

If you had told me four years ago the events and circumstances that would come crashing down around me in just forty-eight months, I never would have believed you.

I could have never anticipated — or even imagined — such things.

It wasn't supposed to be this way. It didn't have to be this way!

But now, there's no denying the backwash of pain and sadness I feel. These aren't the common, garden-variety wounds that we all encounter in the course of life; this is pain that goes bone deep.

So where do we turn when we find ourselves beyond our own ability to cope? What hope do we have that the pain will ever go away?

■ ■ ■ ■

I'm thinking of a family, not so very different from many of the families you know.

Neither rich nor poor, they were respected within the community but not especially well known. The dad in the family was a pastor.

The little girl living under that family's roof was just eight years old on the evening her dad first slipped into her bedroom to do her harm while her mother was out of the house. The sexual abuse that began that night lasted for eight horrible years. The little girl essentially became her dad's slave, always at hand to satisfy his sexual whims.

Her betrayer was her own father. The pastor.

It wasn't supposed to be this way! Fathers are supposed to protect and stand up for their little girls, not molest them, not destroy their lives. She was too young at eight to realize how profoundly her dad had betrayed her — along with her mom and the trusting people of the congregation. But it all came to light when she was sixteen.

(Sixteen . . . isn't that supposed to be a fun, lighthearted time of life?)

In that year, her mother had an affair with

a deacon in the church. And then the whole sad, sordid story about her father's serial sexual abuse was revealed.

Her father went to prison for having sex with a minor — his own daughter. That prison sentence, just and right though it was, only drove the feelings of shame and guilt deeper into the girl's heart. Now her father was in prison *because of her.* And to her disgust, her mother made her socialize with the deacon and his family — as if nothing evil or out of the ordinary had ever happened!

The adults tried to sweep the ugly truth under the rug, but they could not brush away the pain from this sixteen-year-old's heart. The wounds and scars and unanswered questions have left her bitter and confused. Why, why did this happen to her? And what about God? Where does He fit into all of this? Does He even exist? If so, was He too busy or too indifferent to care . . . or too impotent to do anything about it?

Had God betrayed her?

Just a week ago, I received the following e-mail, and my heart just broke for this dear woman:

Dear Kay,

My husband died three years ago . . .

Then three weeks ago my very strongly Christian, happy-go-lucky, nineteen-year-old son committed suicide. He thought he was going to lose his career when he failed a PT test.

I am in despair and clinging to your studies on spiritual warfare, which I know attacked him, and your study on why bad things happen.

Everyone said he was the strongest Christian they knew, so it is almost impossible to understand.

My only other child is a daughter who is eighteen and very ill.

Why do these things happen? I had it all. We were the perfect Christian family, happy, serving God, loving each other. Now we are left with rubble. Does God care?

This woman's questions are the ones we all wrestle with at times in our lives: *Why us? Why now? Does God care?*

Where will she turn for answers, for hope? Where can you and I turn?

I read an article not long ago in *Vanity Fair*

magazine about the family of Bernie Madoff.

Madoff, of course, was the former chairman of the NASDAQ stock exchange and the admitted operator of the Ponzi scheme that has been characterized as the largest investment fraud in Wall Street history. In March of 2009, he pleaded guilty to eleven felonies, admitting to turning his wealth-management business into a scheme that defrauded thousands of investors of billions of dollars.

So much for the headlines; what about the real human lives behind the media frenzy? I want to consider, for a moment, the two young men who also carry the name "Madoff": Mark and Andrew, Bernie's sons.

Were his sons in on the great swindle that swallowed billions of dollars and devastated countless lives? Did they even know what their father was doing? Maybe, and maybe not. But let's just say they *didn't* know. Can you imagine how absolutely humiliated and betrayed they must have felt to learn the truth? Can you begin to gauge the depth of their pain? Their dad — their own father — had done *what?*

Bernie's dramatic confession to his sons on December 10, 2008, would forever alter their lives. Mark was angry; Andrew fell to the floor sobbing. As a consequence, that very afternoon one of those young men picked up the phone and called the Securities and Exchange Commission, setting up an appointment for the next morning.

Can you imagine turning your own father over to the authorities? Maybe you weren't always pleased with him or wished he were different. But it was still *your* father. You bore his name, you loved him, and at one time you were very proud of him.

Maybe you can put yourself in this situation all too well. Perhaps you've uncovered a devastating family secret that forever changed your relationship with a family member, someone you'd previously trusted and respected.

In 2000, according to one source in the magazine article, the Madoff family was a contented lot. Mark Madoff had said it was fun to go to work and find all his family members there working together.

In eight years, however, they went from contentment to sorrow, from prosperity to utter desolation. With each new revelation of their father's unethical and criminal behavior, Mark and Andrew's pain went deeper and deeper.

Take a moment to put yourself in their shoes. These sons claim to have had no part at all in their father's appalling mismanagement and dishonesty. But how many people will look askance at them for the rest of their lives? Can you imagine being totally innocent yet not have others believe you? Maybe you don't have to use your imagination; maybe you've experienced the injustice of having your own reputation tainted by the actions of someone close to you.

And how would you feel knowing that one of your dad's clients committed suicide eleven days after your father's arrest? Before taking an overdose of sleeping pills and slashing his wrists, the distinguished French financier René-Thierry Magon de la Villehuchet, who had invested $1.4 billion with Madoff, wrote in his suicide note, "If you ruin your friends, your clients, you have to face the consequences."[1] Would Madoff's sons feel that blood spill onto their own hands, just because they shared the last name of Madoff?

And what would go through your heart when you thought about all the widows, retirees, charities, and hardworking families who'd lost all their savings because of *your* dad?

Madoff apologized to his victims, saying, "I have left a legacy of shame, as some of my victims have pointed out, to my family and my grandchildren. This is something I will live in for the rest of my life. I'm sorry."

But what about the grandchildren and generations yet to come who will also carry the name "Madoff"?

Story after story could be told of the deep hurts we endure; particularly agonizing are the horrendous accounts of man's inhumanity to man.

And so the questions come . . . for all of us.

Will the pain ever go away?

Is there anything left to hope for? Or is life just about pain?

What do you do, where can you go for help, who can you turn to when the hurt runs deep?

Let's explore those questions together in the pages that follow.

Chapter Two:
You Don't Suffer Alone

How do we cope with the inevitable pain of life in a dark and fallen world so that it doesn't damage us beyond repair or ruin our lives? Are we destined to a future of unrelenting pain, devoid of joy, peace, and satisfaction?

No! I assure you with all my heart that hope, help, and healing are within your reach — and closer at hand than you might have imagined or dreamed. Obviously I wouldn't be writing this book if I didn't believe there was a solution.

I certainly don't claim to have all the answers. Far from it! Even though I may have lived longer than you, I realize I have much to learn. I'm still very much "in process" — just like you.

But even though I don't have all the answers, I know where to find them!

Imagine you bumped into me in a large, unfamiliar airport and asked me how to get to a certain gate. I might know the basic direction, but if we happened to be standing close to an airport information booth, I could do even better than giving you vague or general instructions. I could immediately direct you to a person who stands ready, available, qualified, and motivated to meet your every information need.

In the same way, I know how to direct you to the Source of wisdom and life, healing and hope. And it's my prayer that you will not only "conquer" your hurt, but will come through on the other side, agreeing that, although it was extremely painful, the affliction was worth the end product.

A STORY THAT COULD HELP

Let's go back to that information booth in the busy airport I spoke of a moment ago. Let's say you come to that helper behind the counter in a worried, distracted frame of mind. You're afraid you've already missed your flight. You're not sure you're even in the right terminal. And you have no idea if you have any chance of making it to the right gate in time.

Let's imagine the helper behind the counter says something like this: "May I see your ticket? Okay . . . well, first of all, *you haven't missed your flight.* You can still catch it! And I will tell you exactly what you need to do."

Just knowing that you still have a chance, that there's still hope, can make all the difference. And so it is when we're going through intense pain or grief.

The Bible gives us that reassurance right off the top. The pages of this everlasting book assure us that, no matter where we are, what we have endured, or what we may be facing, there is still hope! We can make it step by step through the difficulties of this life and find lasting happiness and peace in the next life . . . *if* we follow some simple directions.

As it happens, we find one of the most important stories about dealing with personal pain in the very first book of the Bible. It's a story that sets forth a truth, and that truth is then substantiated throughout all sixty-six books of this great book that we know as "God's Word."

I can almost hear your protest: "But, Kay, you have no idea. I've been wounded by Christians . . . by the church . . . by God. If God is God, why would He allow me to go through this pain, this unbearable hurt?"

I understand, and I am so very sorry. However, if you have misunderstood God, or if the churches or people in your past have not represented God correctly, truthfully, and accurately, would you want that misunderstanding or misrepresentation to keep you from knowing what to do when the hurt runs deep? From finding healing and wholeness and hope? Of course not!

And if the Bible holds the key that could unlock your pain and enable you to deal with it — and even come out the better for it — surely you would at least want to listen, to consider what it says, wouldn't you? Of course!

So then, let me take you to the book of Genesis, and to the story of Joseph. Even though you might have heard it before, why don't you try a little experiment? Tell God — right now, out loud — that you want to encounter this story in a way that will bring true and lasting healing into your life.

Do this, *even if you don't believe there is a God.*

Let's read the beginning of Joseph's story. For your convenience, the text from the Bible is printed out below. By the way, do you ever read books with a pencil or pen in hand? I do. Often some thought or question will come to mind, or I'll want to mark something or write a note in the margin or at the top of the page so I can come back and think about what I read. You might want to read this book with pen or pencil in hand.

For instance, as you read the story that follows, you might want to underline everything you learn about Joseph from the Bible. As you read the text, I will "interrupt" from time to time with a few words of explanation about what has gone before, in earlier chapters of Genesis.

And one more thing: sometimes when the Bible is quoted, we think we already know it so we skip over it so we can read the author's words or stories. Please don't! The Bible is as good as it gets. It's absolute truth — God's words! Don't choose man's words over God's words, which can bring such sweet healing. Just watch and see!

SETTING THE SCENE

Now Jacob lived in the land where his father had sojourned, in the land of Canaan. These are the records of the generations of Jacob.

Joseph, when seventeen years of age, was pasturing the flock with his brothers while he was still a youth, along with the sons of Bilhah and the sons of Zilpah, his father's wives. And Joseph brought

23

back a bad report about them to their father. (Genesis 37:1–2)

Back in Genesis 12, God had called Abraham to leave his land and his parents and to go to a land God would show him and eventually give to him as a permanent possession. God also promised to make a great nation from Abraham and to bless all the nations of the earth through Abraham's descendants — which would eventually lead to the birth of Jesus Christ Himself.

That promise of national greatness was confirmed to Abraham's son Isaac and to Isaac's son Jacob. Then God changed Jacob's name to Israel. Are you beginning to get the picture? God was creating a new nation, the nation of Israel. The land that was promised by God was the land of Canaan, later called *Eretz Israel,* the land of Israel.

Jacob had two wives, although he'd contracted for only one. His father-in-law had veiled Leah and sent her into Jacob's tent, when it was her beautiful younger sister, Rachel, Jacob had wanted and worked seven years for. Leah, however, gave Jacob a family, while Rachel remained barren for years.

Finally Rachel herself, the love of Jacob's life, gave birth to Joseph and, later, his younger brother Benjamin. All together,

Jacob fathered twelve sons by two wives and two concubines. These twelve would eventually become the heads of the twelve tribes of Israel, but for now they were all living together in their father's household. Got the picture?

> Now Israel loved Joseph more than all his sons, because he was the son of his old age; and he made him a varicolored tunic. His brothers saw that their father loved him more than all his brothers; and so they hated him and could not speak to him on friendly terms.
> Then Joseph had a dream, and when he told it to his brothers, they hated him even more. (vv. 3–5)

The dream? It was certainly from God, as we will see later. On the surface, it seems from the consequences that it would have been much wiser for Joseph to keep the matter between himself and the Lord. He dreamed of twelve sheaves of grain — obviously corresponding to the twelve sons of Jacob. At some point in the dream, the sheaves associated with his brothers bowed down low to Joseph's sheaf.

Joseph's brothers, of course, immediately picked up the implication — and didn't like it one bit! Already resentful of this pampered "Daddy's favorite," the brothers were deeply offended by Joseph's recitation of the dream.

Then his brothers said to him, "Are you actually going to reign over us? Or are you really going to rule over us?" So they hated him even more for his dreams and for his words. (v. 8)

You would think Joseph might have received the message — his brothers didn't want anything to do with the young man's dreams of future greatness. Yet when Joseph had another such dream, he immediately related it to his family.

"Lo, I have had still another dream; and behold, the sun and the moon and eleven stars were bowing down to me." He related it to his father and to his brothers; and his father rebuked him and said to him, "What is this dream that you have had? Shall I and your mother and your brothers actually come to bow ourselves down before you to the ground?" His brothers were jealous of him, but his father kept the saying in mind. (vv. 9–11)

I know what you're thinking. How naive of this young man to share such dreams with his ten older brothers! It seems like that on the surface, doesn't it? But you won't find the deep answers you're looking for in the Bible by staying on the surface. Joseph will prove to be a deeper young man than we might first imagine.

As Joseph's story progresses, we see that the road soon became very, very difficult for him. He was about to encounter the deepest hurts he had ever experienced in all his young, privileged life.

Jacob (sometimes called Israel) sent Joseph out to check on his older brothers and the condition of the flocks. Little did he realize, as he said good-bye to his son that morning, that he wouldn't see Joseph's face again for *years.*

After looking in vain for his brothers and the family flocks, Joseph finally found them. The Bible doesn't say what Joseph was thinking as he approached his brothers, but it does tell us what his brothers were thinking about *him.* And those thoughts were disturbingly dark.

When they saw him from a distance and before he came close to them, they plotted against him to put him to death.

They said to one another, "Here comes this dreamer! Now then, come and let us kill him and throw him into one of the pits; and we will say, 'A wild beast devoured him.' Then let us see what will become of his dreams!" (vv. 18–20)

Can you relate to the situation Joseph is about to step into? Were you going about your daily life as usual, never suspecting the pain or betrayal that lurked just around the corner?

But Reuben heard this and rescued him out of their hands and said, "Let us not take his life." Reuben further said to them, "Shed no blood. Throw him into this pit that is in the wilderness, but do not lay hands on him" — that he might rescue him out of their hands, to restore him to his father.

So it came about, when Joseph reached his brothers, that they stripped Joseph of his tunic, the varicolored tunic that was on him; and they took him and threw him into the pit. Now the pit was empty, without any water in it.

Then they sat down to eat a meal. (vv. 21–25)

Did you catch those last words? When did

these brothers have lunch together? Right after they tossed their younger brother into a dry pit! I want to share another verse with you that makes clear how deeply traumatic this was for Joseph — and what the brothers remembered about it in later years.

Genesis 42:21–22 describes a scene years later when these very same brothers found themselves in a hard place:

> Then they said to one another, "Truly we are guilty concerning our brother, because we saw the distress of his soul when he pleaded with us, yet we would not listen; therefore this distress has come upon us." Reuben answered them, saying, "Did I not tell you, 'Do not sin against the boy'; and you would not listen? Now comes the reckoning for his blood."

Sometimes we think those who do us wrong are deaf to our cries, to our pleading and begging, because they don't respond. But what we just read tells us that these brothers *had* heard; Joseph's cries had been imprinted on their consciences and memories. And though they undoubtedly tried to push the memory away or forget their little brother through the years, they could never quite erase his pleas and his distress from their minds.

In what these embittered brothers told themselves was an act of mercy, they decided not to kill Joseph outright but rather to sell him to a traveling caravan of Midianites on their way to Egypt. Judah said, "What profit is it for us to kill our brother and cover up his blood? Come and let us sell him to the Ishmaelites and not lay our hands on him, for he is our brother, our own flesh" (Genesis 37:26–27).

But how would they break the news to Jacob, their father? Someone came up with the idea of taking Joseph's tunic — that beautiful garment Jacob himself had made for Joseph — tearing it, and dipping it in goat's blood. Presenting it to their father, they said, "We found this; please examine it to see whether it is your son's tunic or not" (v. 32).

Jacob immediately believed the lie that Joseph had been killed by a wild animal. He went into deep mourning and would not be consoled.

Once a lie is told, it takes a mountain of courage to confess it, doesn't it? It's difficult to admit you were wrong, or that you acted out of jealousy. None of Jacob's sons had that sort of courage. They had heard the frantic pleadings of Joseph, and now they witnessed the overwhelming sorrow and tears of their father. Even so, they held on to their lie. *"That's our story, and we're stickin' to it."*

Meanwhile, what happened to Joseph?

Scripture says: "Meanwhile, the Midianites sold him in Egypt to Potiphar, Pharaoh's officer, the captain of the bodyguard" (v. 36).

Have you ever found yourself alone, abandoned, and in a strange place? That's how it was for this young teenager who had been betrayed and sold by his own brothers. *How could it happen? Life isn't supposed to work that way . . . is it?*

Let's follow Joseph to Egypt.

TWISTS AND TURNS

Whether you're encountering this story for the first time or the hundred-and-first time, you can't help but be amazed by all the intriguing twists and turns in this real-life account.

If this were a purely human story, you might expect things to go from bad to worse for this young man. But the Bible isn't just a collection of historical accounts; it is *His* story. And when God is involved in a situation, you can throw out all the common expectations. In fact, Scripture tells us that "the LORD was with Joseph, so he became a successful man" (Genesis 39:2).

A successful man? After being sold as a slave in Egypt? How could that be? Very simply, when God steps into the picture, every equation changes. As a result, then . . .

> . . . His master saw that the LORD was with him and how the LORD caused all that he did to prosper in his hand. So Joseph found favor in his sight and became his personal servant; and he made him overseer over his house, and all that he owned he put in his charge. It came about that from the time he made him overseer in his house and over all that he owned, the LORD blessed the Egyptian's house on account of Joseph; thus the LORD's blessing was upon all that he owned, in the house and in the field. (vv. 3–5)

Did Joseph think he was alone in Egypt? The text doesn't tell us. We can make a guess, perhaps, but that's a detail God hasn't chosen to reveal. What we can know for sure is that the Lord was with Joseph — and just as surely, He is with you, no matter how abandoned you may feel right now.

That's the fact God wants you to see; that's the point He doesn't want you to miss, so keep it in mind as we read the next twist in the story.

> Now Joseph was handsome in form and appearance. It came about after these events that his master's wife looked with desire at Joseph, and she said, "Lie with me."
>
> But he refused and said to his master's wife, "Behold, with me here, my master does not concern himself with anything in the house, and he has put all that he owns in my charge. There is no one greater in this house than I, and he has withheld nothing from me except you, because you are his wife. How then could I do this great evil and sin against God?"
>
> As she spoke to Joseph day after day, he did not listen to her to lie beside her or be with her. (vv. 6–10)

We could easily skip past that little phrase "day after day." It means over and over and over again. Potiphar's wife didn't proposition Joseph once, but *many* times. We can only imagine how she used all her feminine wiles to distract, confuse, and seduce this young man, seeking to wear down his resistance. But Joseph stayed faithful — to his master and to his Lord.

Now it happened one day that he went into the house to do his work, and none of the men of the household was there inside. She caught him by his garment, saying, "Lie with me!" And he left his garment in her hand and fled, and went outside. (vv. 11–12)

Was Joseph still a young man of integrity? Yes! But even though Potiphar had done well picking a good slave, this story makes it clear he hadn't done so well in picking a good woman.

The Genesis account goes on to describe how Potiphar's wife, her pride no doubt stung by this slave's blunt refusal of her favors, made the outlandish claim that Joseph had attempted to rape her. By the time her husband got home that night, she had her story down pat. The Egyptian official had no choice but to have Joseph arrested.

So Joseph's master took him and put him into the jail, the place where the king's prisoners were confined; and he was there in the jail. (v. 20)

How could this happen? This wasn't right! It wasn't fair! Joseph didn't deserve that sort of treatment. Hadn't he done what was right and honorable? And now he was in jail. Where was God in all this? Had the Lord deserted him in this new crisis?

Far from it! Once again we read that "the LORD was with Joseph and extended kindness to him, and gave him favor in the sight of the chief jailer" (v. 21). As a result, the chief jailer ended up turning over the operation of the whole prison to this young Hebrew slave. And everything began to run smoothly from that day forward. The favor of God changes everything!

These events set up an interesting encounter between Joseph and two of the inmates:

Then it came about after these things, the cupbearer and the baker for the king of Egypt offended their lord, the king of Egypt. Pharaoh was furious with his two officials, the chief cupbearer and the chief baker. So he put them in confinement in the house of the captain of the bodyguard, in the jail, the same place where Joseph was imprisoned. The captain of the bodyguard put Joseph in charge of them, and he took care of them; and they were in confinement for some time. Then the cupbearer and the baker for the king of Egypt, who were confined in jail, both had a dream the same night, each man with his own dream and each dream with its own interpretation.

When Joseph came to them in the morning and observed them, behold, they were dejected. He asked Pharaoh's officials who were with him in confinement in his master's house, "Why are your faces so sad today?" Then they said to him, "We have had a dream and there is no one to interpret it." Then Joseph said to them, "Do not interpretations belong to God? Tell it to me, please." (Genesis 40:1–8)

So the chief cupbearer and the chief baker both described their dreams to Joseph. Interpreting the details of each, he explained that in three days' time the baker would be hanged while the cupbearer would be restored to his office. And Joseph made this request of the cupbearer:

"Only keep me in mind when it goes well with you, and please do me a kindness by mentioning me to Pharaoh and get me out of this house. For I was in fact kidnapped from the land of the Hebrews, and even here I have done nothing that they should have put me into the dungeon." (vv. 14–15)

It all took place just as Joseph had said. After three days, Pharaoh honored the chief cupbearer and restored him to his office, and he hanged the chief baker. You would think the cupbearer would have had reason to remember Joseph and speak a word in his behalf. But he didn't. Scripture tells us, "The chief cupbearer did not remember Joseph, but forgot him" (v. 23).

What sad words! Yes, the Lord was with Joseph even in prison. But it wasn't where Joseph wanted to be, was it? As it turned out, Joseph would be in that dungeon another *two years.*

His hoped-for ticket out of maximum security didn't materialize, and we can imagine him wondering if things would *ever* change. Was he doomed to permanent disappointment? Had God forgotten about him too?

Maybe you can relate to this portion of Joseph's story. Put the book down and think about it, maybe taking a minute to write out your thoughts in the margin. In the next chapter we'll get to the fundamental truth that unlocks the door to hurt, enabling you to (finally) heal.

CHAPTER THREE:
IS THERE PURPOSE
IN YOUR PAIN?

Here is how it is with us when the heart-aches of life muscle in and take over.

We cry, plead, wring our hands, or bite our nails. We pull the shades, draw the curtains, lock the doors, turn off the lights, get into bed, pull the covers over our head, and roll ourselves into a ball — or at least we want to. We tell ourselves, "I'm the only one I have to hang on to!" We feel guilty, worthless, helpless, hopeless — and perhaps angry.

Maybe we turn to something near at hand for comfort, like food, drugs, or alcohol. Or we run into the arms of anyone who will hold us and say they love us. Anything, we tell ourselves, is better than being alone in our pain.

And somewhere in the process, we pray. It's usually after we've finally concluded that nothing on earth will really help us. So we cry out in the hope that there is a divine being out there . . . somewhere . . . who can come to our aid.

But what then? When God seemingly doesn't hear, doesn't answer, doesn't move in His supposedly divine power to rescue us from our pain, we assume we're unworthy of His notice or that He really doesn't care.

Or that He's not even there at all.

And so we either forget God or assume He has forgotten us. We begin groping in the dark, like a blind person trying to get his bearings in an unfamiliar place. We try to find our own way to cope, to survive.

So is survival the best we can hope for?

My friend, I truly believe we don't have to settle for surviving; we can find genuine healing for our hurts, and that's what this book is all about. I've had this book in my heart for a long, long time, and as I reflect on it now, I honestly feel that this is one of the very purposes for my life: to tell you about the One who heals, comforts, and rescues lives from darkness and despair.

But I need you to stay with me, all the way through, because we have a lot of ground to cover. God never promises an instant cure to anyone, but He will be a light in the darkness and a strong guiding hand to everyone who calls on Him. Hang in there, dear reader, and your life *will* begin to change!

MEANWHILE, BACK IN THE DUNGEON . . .

Now then, with that said, let's return to Joseph, seemingly forgotten in prison. He may be running the place, but prison is still prison. And it's been *two long years* since the forgetful cupbearer was set free.

What about those dreams, Joseph?

What about your brothers' sheaves of grain bowing down to yours? What about your mother and father bowing down? Were these dreams really from God? Could God be trusted? By this time, it had been years — long, lonely years — since Joseph had seen his family.

We know that God had not abandoned Joseph, because we find in the book of Psalms a passage that reveals God had a plan and a wonderful destiny for Joseph right from the beginning, and right through all his hurts and sorrows.

And He [God] called for a famine upon
  the land;
  He broke the whole staff of bread.
He sent a man before them,
  Joseph, who was sold as a slave.

41

They afflicted his feet with fetters,
    He himself was laid in irons;
Until the time that his word came to
    pass,
    The word of the LORD tested him.
The king sent and released him,
    The ruler of peoples, and set him free.
He made him lord of his house
    And ruler over all his possessions,
To imprison his princes at will,
    That he might teach his elders wisdom.
    (Psalm 105:16–22)

Did you get that? It was God who had called for a famine on the land of Israel. And it was God who sent a man before Jacob and his sons, so they would have food to eat in the famine! But Joseph wasn't sent as an ambassador, he was sent as a *slave.* In shame and degradation. In humiliation and hurt. His legs were put in rusty iron bands and connected with chains that scraped his young flesh.

Joseph didn't have any idea what was happening behind the scenes, because at that point God hadn't told him. All he had to cling to through all his trials and troubles were the two extremely vivid dreams he'd had as a teenager back in Canaan to assure him that someday, somehow, he would triumph.

But that triumph had to wait on God's timing, until "the word of the LORD tested him." Don't miss that! The word of the Lord was testing Joseph. Would Joseph believe God? Cling to Him? Persevere? Or would he let his pain or circumstances shape who he was? Would he give in to anger, bitterness, cynicism?

The Bible has the answer to those questions, and you can read the remaining story for yourself in Genesis 41–50. For now, however, let me give you the highlights.

Two years after the chief cupbearer was restored to his previous position, Pharaoh had a disturbing dream. The next morning he was so troubled that he called in all the wise men of the nation, but none of them could interpret his dream. At long last, the cupbearer remembered poor Joseph, and he described to Pharaoh how the young prisoner had accurately interpreted his dream, as well as that of the chief baker.

Then Pharaoh sent and called for Joseph, and they hurriedly brought him out of the dungeon; and when he had shaved himself and changed his clothes, he came to Pharaoh. Pharaoh said to Joseph, "I have had a dream, but no one can interpret it; and I have heard it said about you, that when you hear a dream you can interpret it." Joseph then answered Pharaoh, saying, "It is not in me; God will give Pharaoh a favorable answer." (Genesis 41:14–16)

Pharaoh then described his dream, in which seven scrawny cows devoured seven fat cows, then seven withered ears of corn sprouted and swallowed seven full ears of corn. Since none of his magicians could explain the meaning of these disturbing images, you can imagine how eager he was to hear what Joseph would say.

Remember to watch carefully Joseph's words in these next few verses. This is the moment you might expect Joseph's hurt and bitterness over his unfair treatment to come spilling out — including any resentment he felt toward the Lord. If you see any mention of God, you might want to underline it.

Now Joseph said to Pharaoh, "Pharaoh's dreams are one and the same; God has told to Pharaoh what He is about to do. The seven good cows are seven years; and the seven good ears are seven years;

the dreams are one and the same. The seven lean and ugly cows that came up after them are seven years, and the seven thin ears scorched by the east wind will be seven years of famine. It is as I have spoken to Pharaoh: God has shown to Pharaoh what He is about to do. Behold, seven years of great abundance are coming in all the land of Egypt; and after them seven years of famine will come, and all the abundance will be forgotten in the land of Egypt, and the famine will ravage the land. So the abundance will be unknown in the land because of that subsequent famine; for it will be very severe. Now as for the repeating of the dream to Pharaoh twice, it means that the matter is determined by God, and God will quickly bring it about. Now let Pharaoh look for a man discerning and wise, and set him over the land of Egypt. Let Pharaoh take action to appoint overseers in charge of the land, and let him exact a fifth of the produce of the land of Egypt in the seven years of abundance. Then let them gather all the food of these good years that are coming, and store up the grain for food in the cities under Pharaoh's authority, and let them guard it. Let the food become as a reserve for the land for the seven years of famine which will occur in the land of Egypt, so that the land will not perish during the famine."

Now the proposal seemed good to Pharaoh and to all his servants. (vv. 25–37)

What do you think? Does it sound as if Joseph thought God was controlling the crops? Bringing plenty and then following it with famine? Did God have anything to do with famines? How did Pharaoh respond to this young man's bold proposal?

Nicer conditions in the dungeon, perhaps? Maybe a reduced sentence? An extra food allowance? Not even close! As I said earlier, when God gets involved in a situation, He has the power to change *everything.*

So Pharaoh said to Joseph, "Since God has informed you of all this, there is no one so discerning and wise as you are. You shall be over my house, and according to your command all my people shall do homage; only in the throne I will be greater than you." . . .

Then Pharaoh took off his signet ring from his hand and put it on Joseph's hand, and clothed him in garments of fine linen and put the gold necklace around his neck. He had him ride in his second chariot; and they proclaimed before him, "Bow the knee!" And he set him over all the land of Egypt. Moreover, Pharaoh said to Joseph, "Though I am Pharaoh, yet without your permission no one shall raise his hand or foot in all the land of Egypt." (vv. 39–44)

Pharaoh was so impressed by Joseph's wisdom and discernment, he named him second-in-command for the whole nation of Egypt. Joseph had gone from being Jacob's pet . . . to a pit . . . to Potiphar's . . . to a prison . . . to a palace! Which is exactly what God intended for him all along! Granted, it was a circuitous route with plenty of unhappy, puzzling twists and turns, but it was *God's* route.

THE UNSEEN POWER AT WORK

The dreams God gave a young lad of seventeen and that he shared with his brothers and his father were about to come to pass — in a way beyond anything Joseph could have imagined.

And how did it all come about? Was it coincidence? Fate? Or was it God?

You already know it was God, because you

read about His plans in Psalm 105. But that was revealed much later, written for the benefit of later generations. Joseph didn't have that piece of information, so what explanation did he give for this whole stunning turn of events? His answer is very, very important, *because within his answer lies the key truth that unlocks the power to heal.*

Through an utterly amazing set of circumstances (which are so worth your time to read in full in Genesis 42–45), Joseph came face to face with the brothers who had betrayed him and sold him into slavery. They came from Canaan to Egypt to buy grain, so the family could survive the famine that came just as God had forewarned through Pharaoh's dream.

Remember the dream of the sheaves? It came to life right before Joseph's eyes as his brothers, not recognizing him, bowed low in his presence.

Let's look at Genesis 45. As you do, watch Joseph . . . and see if his hurt ran deep.

Then Joseph could not control himself before all those who stood by him, and he cried, "Have everyone go out from me." So there was no man with him when Joseph made himself known to his brothers. He wept so loudly that the

Egyptians heard it, and the household of Pharaoh heard of it. Then Joseph said to his brothers, "I am Joseph! Is my father still alive?" But his brothers could not answer him, for they were dismayed at his presence.

Then Joseph said to his brothers, "Please come closer to me." And they came closer. And he said, "I am your brother Joseph, whom you sold into Egypt." (vv. 1–4)

Stop for a minute and think about what Joseph had been through. Consider everything that had happened to him because of the cold-hearted jealousy and hatred of his brothers. They had even thought of killing him outright!

And now . . . how would Joseph respond to them?

"Now do not be grieved or angry with yourselves, because you sold me here, for God sent me before you to preserve life. For the famine has been in the land these two years, and there are still five years in which there will be neither plowing nor harvesting. God sent me before you to preserve for you a remnant in the earth, and to keep you alive by a great deliverance. Now, therefore, it was not you who sent me here, but God; and He has made me a father to Pharaoh and lord of all his household and ruler over all the land of Egypt." (vv. 5–8)

What is God telling you as you consider Joseph's words? God's words are for the healing of His people. What truths can you grab on to that will help you when the hurt runs deep? Have you got your pencil or pen? Read those verses again and underline every reference to God, including any "He" in verses 5–8. What do you learn about God? Think, take it in, savor it, and meditate on it. Read this passage aloud several times and let the words penetrate deep into the creases and crevices of your soul.

GOD IS IN THE DETAILS

Joseph sent his brothers on their way home to pick up Jacob and bring the rest of the family and all the livestock down to Egypt. He said, in effect, "Tell Dad all about my new position — and hurry back!"

As you continue in Genesis, you'll read about Jacob's trip to Egypt — and God's specific word of comfort to him on the way. Jacob knew he would die a contented man, if only he could see his beloved and long-lost son once again.

And what about the brothers? Do you think that those who do wrong, those who inflict pain on others, experience hurt of their own? Does guilt trouble their thoughts or conscience? I think it depends on what they have done to their conscience — whether or not they have disabled it by choosing to do wrong over and over, excusing themselves with every repetition of sin until they become inoculated against guilt. If that's the case, their evil only escalates until they feel nothing at all. And sooner or later they begin to reap the awful harvest of their gruesome acts of rebellion against God.

From what we saw in the previous chapter, we know Joseph's brothers were troubled by their sin and — deep down — knew God would justly judge them. Their consciences had not been totally disabled. Remember their conversation before the second-in-command over Egypt revealed his identity as their brother? "Truly we are guilty concerning our brother, because we saw the distress of his soul when he pleaded with us, yet we would not listen; therefore this distress has come upon us" (Genesis 42:21).

And how did Reuben respond? "Did I not tell you, 'Do not sin against the boy';

and . . . now comes the reckoning for his blood" (v. 22).

After their father, Jacob, died, once again the brothers began to tremble with fear. What if Joseph had only spared them for their father's sake? It was hard for them to grasp the depth of Joseph's trust in God's supreme authority and power — His rule over all.

So how did Joseph respond to their fear of retaliation now that Dad was gone? Listen for the priceless truth in these words: "As for you, you meant evil against me, *but God meant it for good* in order to bring about this present result, to preserve many people alive" (Genesis 50:20).

HEALING TRUTH #1

If God has allowed pain in our lives, He has allowed it for a purpose — a good purpose, because He is a good God.

Be sure you don't miss the healing truth tucked within his words, precious one.

Joseph didn't gloss over or deny the wrongness of his brothers' actions and the evil they had perpetrated. He let them know their behavior was truly evil. But Joseph also knew that God rules in the affairs of man . . . and that his pain had a purpose.

So does yours, beloved of God. If it didn't, God would not have allowed it. God is sovereign. You may not be able to see it now, but just as God worked through Joseph's circumstances to bring about His ultimate purposes, so He will work in your life, if you will trust Him with the outcome.

In the pages ahead we'll take a closer look at how the fact that God is sovereign can bring hope and healing amid our pain. Meanwhile, as you end this chapter, stop and think about what you've learned from the story of Joseph. No matter how hard it may be to believe right now, you are not alone in your pain; God is with you. And somehow — often in ways we can't even begin to imagine — He can work good out of the darkest circumstances.

CHAPTER FOUR:
WHAT KIND OF GOD
ALLOWS OUR PAIN?

When I speak of the sovereignty of God and tell you that it's the very key that unlocks and heals our hurts, what do I mean?

It's important that we define our terms, especially because *sovereign* isn't a word most of us toss around in everyday conversation!

From first to last, the Bible tells us God is sovereign; He holds supreme authority over absolutely everything and everyone. The very first book of the Bible begins with God speaking the simple words "Let there be" — and immediately "it was so." He spoke the world and man into existence. And the Bible concludes with the strong message that God overrules the evil of men and will ultimately bring His good purposes to pass:

I heard a loud voice from the throne, saying, "Behold, the tabernacle of God is among men, and He will dwell among them, and they shall be His people, and God Himself will be among them, and He will wipe away every tear from their eyes; and there will no longer be any death; there will no longer be any mourning, or crying, or pain; the first things have passed away."

And He who sits on the throne said, "Behold, I am making all things new." (Revelation 21:3–5)

Every page in between reaffirms that the Creator of the heavens and the earth has it all under control . . . even when the hurt runs deep.

Man wants to think *he's* in charge, and that he has the first and last word about everything. But it isn't true. That sort of man-centered thinking has brought us into a world of hurt — literally!

Many people like the idea of having God or a "higher power" around when it suits them, to help them with their stuff as long as He doesn't interfere. In other words, "God is all right as long as He doesn't make any demands on my life, talk to me about my lifestyle, or get in the way of anything I want to plan or do. It's fine if He stays in the background — kind of a jolly old grandfather in the sky who lets me do whatever I want and never gets in my way."

That may be the view some people have of God, but that is *not* the God of the Bible.

What mankind doesn't realize (or refuses to acknowledge) is that man did not create or invent God. Rather, it was God who created man, and no one knows better than He about how human life should work.

I am pausing to say all this because I firmly believe that genuine healing is tied to a correct knowledge of God's sovereignty — His rule over everything — and His character.

HEALING TRUTH #2

Deep and genuine healing will always be tied to an accurate knowledge of God's sovereignty and character. The clearer our understanding of who God is, the more profound our healing will be.

So let's give the Word of God a hearing.

There are really only two choices in life: the word of man — what man says, thinks, and believes — or the Word of God — what God says and has caused to be written in the Bible.

We all know where the word of man has led us: a dark dead end of hurt and despair.

So let's continue together through these pages to see what the Word of God has to say about life and about healing for our heartaches and troubles.

It will be an adventure . . . and we'll be traveling the path together all the way. Remember that my hurt, too, has run very deep.

In Psalm 103:19 we read, "His sovereignty rules over all." Do you see the word *reign* toward the end of sovereignty? To reign is to rule. When we say God is sovereign, it means He rules over e-v-e-r-y-t-h-i-n-g. *Everything.* His sovereignty is a truth you see explained and demonstrated repeatedly throughout the Bible.

Before we go any further, let's take a closer look at the Book which teaches us so clearly and plainly about a God who rules — right down to the teeny-tiny details of our lives.

SOVEREIGN GOD, SOVEREIGN BOOK

Christians generally believe the Bible includes both an Old and a New Testament.

If you are Jewish, the term *Bible* refers to what Christians call the Old Testament, Genesis through Malachi. Those who don't know the Old Testament are truly spiritually impoverished. It is there you meet God, learn His ways, discover His character, and understand His sovereignty as He demonstrates it over and over again — over man, animals, nature, nations, life, death, and destiny. I truly don't believe you can have an adequate knowledge of God without knowing the Old Testament.

As you read the New Testament, you find it constantly quoting or referring to the Old Testament. Why? Among other reasons, it's because 333 Old Testament promises about the coming Messiah are fulfilled in the person of Jesus Christ and in His first coming to earth.

The New Testament begins with the four Gospel accounts of the life of Messiah, the Christ, followed by His death, burial, resurrection, and the commissioning of those who believe to go into the world and make followers of Jesus Christ. This is followed by the book of Acts, which gives a historical account of the early followers of Jesus Christ . . . who came to be known as "Christians," or "little Christs."

The Gospels and the book of Acts are then followed by letters of various lengths that explain what Christ-followers are to believe and how we are to live in the light of those truths.

The final book of the New Testament is

the book of Revelation, which contains the unveiling of things yet to come upon the earth. Revelation gives us an astonishing picture of the times preceding the return of Jesus Christ, when He will demolish all other kingdoms and reign on the earth as King of kings and Lord of lords. (No one will question God's sovereignty in that day!) The account of His second coming is recorded in Revelation 19.

In Revelation 20 we're told what happens after that. We will all live forever, either with God and His Son in heaven or with the devil and his angels in the lake of fire.

Chapters 21 and 22 of Revelation describe to us a new heaven, a new earth, and the heavenly Jerusalem. It's not only fascinating; it is breathtaking. It ends with these words: "He who testifies to these things says, 'Yes, I am coming quickly.' Amen. Come, Lord Jesus. The grace of the Lord Jesus be with all. Amen" (Revelation 22:20–21).

Now, think with me for a minute: how can God have all sixty-six books of the Bible written by more than forty authors from various walks of life over a period of approximately 1,400 to 1,800 years — without contradictions — and line up the whole world so that it all happens just as He said it would?

It's because He is God. And because He is God, He is sovereign.

But this brings us to a new question: if a sovereign God truly is in control of this world, can He be trusted to act in our best interests? Or are we at the mercy of a despot who couldn't care less what happens to us?

UNCONDITIONAL LOVE

All my life all I wanted was a man who would love me unconditionally. Pretty or ugly, sick or healthy, rich or poor — I wanted to know he would love me no matter what.

My first marriage ended in divorce. I was just twenty-six and the mother of two boys.

Following that devastating experience, I stood in the living room of my apartment, shook my fist in the face of God, and said, "To hell with You, God. I'm going to find somebody to love me." And of course you probably know where I went after that — from one man to another.

HEALING TRUTH #3

Because God is love, and because God rules over all, everything that comes into

60

our lives is filtered through His sovereign
fingers of love.

Finally at age twenty-nine I met the One who would love me unconditionally. His name is Jesus. He is the Son of God, and His Father became my Father.

Oh, my friend, how I wish I could sit with you and look into your eyes so you know how deeply I believe this truth, even in the face of all the trials that have come to me in the past few years: our God can be trusted, without reservation, because He loves us with an everlasting love.[1]

I think one of the most important truths we need to grasp about the One who rules over all is that He is love. And because He is love and He is sovereign, everything that comes into our lives is filtered through His fingers of love.

God loves because He is love. Listen to what He says in His book and wants you and the world to know. Read it aloud so you hear it.

Beloved, let us love one another, for love is from God; and everyone who loves is born of God and knows God. The one who does not love does not know God, for God is love. By this the love of God was manifested in us, that God has sent His only begotten Son into the world so that we might live through Him. (1 John 4:7–9)

Did you hear the word *love* repeated over and over? Got your pencil or pen? Why don't you draw a little heart over every mention of love.

Now let's break this passage down to its basic components to see what we can learn.

We are to love one another. Think of what would happen to all the hurt in the world around us if we really loved one another. Hurt wouldn't be as rampant as it is, would it? Of course it would happen, because we aren't perfect, but love would correct it.

Love is from God. That's interesting, isn't it? God is the source, the well of love.

Those who love (the word means "to desire another's highest good") are born of God. In other words, they have become God's children. The fact that they love shows they truly know God and are part of His family.

Those who do not love, don't know God.

God IS love. Love has its source in Him.

God's love is manifested — demonstrated — in us, because God sent His only begotten Son, Jesus, into the world for us. In other words, you know you are loved because of what God did for you: He sent Jesus into the world so that you might not die and go to hell, but believe and live with God forever.

Now catch what is said in 1 John 4:19: "We love, because He first loved us."

Think about it. Don't just read words; let their truth sink in. God loved you first! *First.* You only love because God loved you first!

LOVE THAT WILL NEVER LET YOU GO
Perhaps you are thinking something like this: *Kay, I just don't get it. If God is love and He loves me, then why don't I see or feel that love? Honestly, given the agony I'm in, it feels more like God doesn't even like me.*

Nevertheless, whether we feel God's love or not, it is one of the greatest realities of our existence. Listen to Romans 5:

> While we were still helpless, at the right time Christ died for the ungodly. For one will hardly die for a righteous man; though perhaps for the good man someone would dare even to die. But God demonstrates His own love toward us, in that while we were yet sinners, Christ died for us. Much more then, having now been justified by His blood, we shall be saved from the wrath of God through

Him. For if while we were enemies we were reconciled to God through the death of His Son, much more, having been reconciled, we shall be saved by His life. (vv. 6–10)

Read it again and see how we are described: "helpless" (v. 6), "sinners" (v. 8), "enemies" (v. 10). And *this* is when God demonstrated His love for us. We were headed for wrath, and Jesus Christ died for us. He justified us, paying the penalty for our sins so we could be forgiven and declared right with God. God reconciled us to Himself when we were His enemies and helpless sinners. It wasn't *after* we got cleaned up, got our lives together, and made ourselves acceptable. No, it was when we were in rebellion — as when I shook my fist in the face of God and said, "To hell with You, God." And that's exactly what Jesus did. He died and took my "hell," my punishment, so that I could have His life!

We who were dead because of our sins, our rebellion against the truth of God's Word, can move from death to life by believing in and receiving Jesus. "But as many as received Him, to them He gave the right to become children of God, even to those who believe in His name" (John 1:12).

Have you ever seen advertisements around ball fields or on signs or bumper stickers that say "John 3:16"? If anyone would notice such a sign and actually go to a Bible to look up that reference, he would read: "For God so loved the world, that He gave His only begotten Son, that whoever believes in Him shall not perish, but have eternal life."

This is love: that God would actually allow His own Son to be sacrificed — put to death — *in your place.* God had Jesus pay for your sins (your unbelief and rebellion against His commandments) so that you would not perish (go to hell and live forever in eternal pain in the lake of fire). He did this so He could offer you eternal life, a forever home in heaven with Him and with His Son whom He raised from the dead.

Have you got it? Do you understand? Do you believe it? If so, you are on your way to handling the hurt that runs so deep.

CHAPTER FIVE:
A FRIEND IN HIGH PLACES

Several weeks ago I informed my Facebook friends that I was writing a book titled *When the Hurt Runs Deep.* Not only did I ask them to pray for me as I completed this project, but I also asked them to share some of their own stories with me. What sorts of questions — and answers — did they encounter in those times of darkness and pain in their own lives?

A number of friends willingly shared lessons learned and insights gained in those difficult, heartbreaking days of deep hurt. What surprised me most, however, was the way my friends kept bringing up the sovereignty of God. In story after story, they mentioned the value and the healing power of gaining a more accurate understanding of God's character, power, and love.

THE BIBLE IN ONE WORD

In John 10 Jesus assured God's sheep (those who believe in Him) that God holds them in His hand, and that no one can ever pluck them out of it.

God's love and power to keep us in His hand is seen in His redemption. *Redemption* isn't a term we use a whole lot, except perhaps when it comes to redeeming coupons in a store. However, the words *redemption, redeem,* and *redeemer* play a critical role in the Bible.

To "redeem" means to purchase or buy back. While the basic meaning stays the same, the references to redemption in the Bible carry different nuances according to how the word is used in a particular text. For instance, one use of the term in the Bible refers to purchasing a slave and then setting him free so he could never again be sold into slavery.

If you've ever wanted to know what the Bible was all about in a single word, *redemption* pretty well sums it all up. In the very first book of the Bible, God promises a redeemer who will crush the head of the lying, murderous serpent.[1] The rest of the Old Testament testifies over and over of the Anointed One who will come to redeem man from the wages of sin — which is death, eternal separation from God. Over and over again, God promised a Messiah who would provide forgiveness of sins for those who call on Him and enable us to live in obedience to God.

And who is this One who can accomplish such things? Not only is He a God who is love, He is an *omnipotent,* or all-powerful, God. A God who can do anything. Nothing is too difficult for the One who by His very word created the world and all that is in it!

He is *omniscient,* or all-knowing. Knowledge and wisdom belong to Him. There is nothing that God does not know. God cannot be blindsided! Does that comfort you? It should, because it means He knows the very source of your hurt, your deepest pain. He knows exactly how to touch it, heal it, and use it to bring about your highest good — to make you more like Jesus. Nothing is unknown with God.

HEALING TRUTH #4

Because God is all-knowing, He knows the very source of your deepest pain — and He understands exactly how to touch it, heal it, and use it to bring about your highest good.

He is *omnipresent,* or everywhere at once. There is nowhere in the universe where He is not! The darkness can't hide things from Him, He sees to the lowest depths of the seas. Man can't hide from Him, because His eyes see through every wall, every hiding place, every deception. His name is El Roi, the God who sees.[2]

God saw what was done to you in the dark, that no one else saw. God heard what was said to you behind closed doors, that no one else heard. He is Truth itself and dwells in a resplendent sea of light. None can hide from the presence of God. No one can overpower Him or get a "one up" on Him.

As you move through the Old Testament, you learn that the Sovereign God is merciful, long-suffering, and compassionate. He is patient and kind in His dealings with us — but deal with us He will. He *has* to, because He is righteous. In other words He is right, does what is right, says what is right, and commands what is right. He never does what is wrong; He is righteous in all His ways and actions. He is just, the righteous Judge, without the tiniest hint or shadow of injustice.

A JUST JUDGE

Maybe at some point in your life you have stood before someone who judged you unjustly and you felt helpless in the face of such undeserved condemnation. But there is a Judge who sits above them all, and no one overturns His decisions. He knows all, sees all, understands all, and will justly repay the ungodly for all their ungodly deeds. He is the judge of all the earth, and one day He will deal out just retribution to those who have rejected His Son and turned their backs on His ways.[3]

You may not see justice now, next week, or even next year, but you can know for sure that judgment and justice are coming. God is love, yes, but He is also *holy.* That means He is set apart, different from man, absolutely right and absolutely righteous. His holiness and His righteousness command His wrath — His righteous anger against all that is opposed to Him and to His Word. For this reason, He is also known as a God of wrath — of righteous indignation and just judgment.

And what does that mean to you, you who are hurting? How does that help? It means this: your hurt *will* be accounted for and taken care of. It will be dealt with justly in God's time and in God's way.

And how can He do that? Read Daniel 4:34–35 and you will see again that He is sovereign and that He rules — not only over all the angelic beings, but also over Satan and his fallen angels. He rules over all the inhabitants of the earth. All human beings, no matter how much they may be used or controlled by their flesh, are ultimately under God's dominion. No one can stop God's hand, beloved. No one can call God into court and ask Him what He is doing. God is not answerable to man. Rather, man is answerable to God.

If, however, you belong to this great and mighty God, if you have been born into His family by believing in and receiving Jesus Christ, then God has a promise for you, His child. The promise is recorded in Romans 8:28–32. Please read these magnificent words right out loud, so that you can hear them with your own ears. And if you have your pencil in hand, underline every *those, these,* and *us.*

And we know that God causes all things to work together for good to those who love God, to those who are called according to His purpose. For those whom He foreknew, He also predestined to become conformed to the image of His

Son, so that He would be the firstborn among many brethren; and these whom He predestined, He also called; and these whom He called, He also justified; and these whom He justified, He also glorified.

What then shall we say to these things? If God is for us, who is against us? He who did not spare His own Son, but delivered Him over for us all, how will He not also with Him freely give us all things?

Did you see it, dear friend? Have you discovered God's promise to you?

GOD'S PROMISE IN THE MIDST OF YOUR PAIN

Please look back again at those wonderful words, and together let's dig a little deeper to see what we can learn about the words *those, these,* and *us.*

First, this is a promise to "those who love God." It's a promise that God will cause all things (all without exception, the good, the bad, and the ugly) to keep on working together for good. The verb form is in the present tense in the original language, which indicates continuous or habitual action and could be translated "to keep on working together for good."

Please note that this passage does *not* say that all things are good.

We know they're not. Some things we encounter in our lives are utterly evil, through and through. No, all things are not good, but God promises that all things will *turn out* for your ultimate good. Some of that benefit may be in this life, and much will certainly be in the next life. Nevertheless, these hurts, failures, and heartaches *will* be used to accomplish God's purpose for you. And what is that purpose? According to verse 29, it is to make you like Jesus Christ. I have always loved this passage for its wonderful assurance that if you are God's child and you love Him, *all* things will turn out for your ultimate good.

Second, according to verse 29, God foreknew you. In other words, you are not a surprise to God. Nothing about you surprises Him or takes Him aback.

Psalm 139 says that God Himself formed you in your mother's womb. God knew who your mama and papa would be. He knew the exact sperm and the precise egg that would come together to make you who you are. He designed you, planned the day of your birth, and knows exactly how long you will live on this earth, down to the very second.

Of course He does. He's sovereign! He rules over all! Read Psalm 139; it's all there.

Third, from the very beginning, God has destined you to be like Jesus. God predestined Christlikeness for you, the process of moving you along from a sinner to a saint. (Don't be alarmed by that word *saint.* It simply means a person set apart for God. All Christians are called saints in the New Testament.) Romans 8:30 says He predestined, marked out beforehand, for you to be like His Son. And how does God do this? By the circumstances of your birth and the things and people He permits into your life . . . *even the hurt!*

Please hear these words, beloved: *if you are a child of God or become one, the hurt that runs deep has a purpose.*

Really? Yes. He will use any and every hurt in your life, even those hurts that came into your life before you became a true Christian.

God is going to use them —
      no matter how hellish,
      how horrific,
      how atrocious,
      how vicious,
      or how seemingly destructive or devastating —

to make you like Jesus.

Fourth, Jesus paid all your debt. According to verse 30, you are not only predestined by God but called by God and justified by God. To justify means to declare you righteous before God, or put you in right standing with Him. God can do that because Jesus paid for all your sins in full, granting you complete forgiveness. Jesus paid your debt, picking up the bill for every single one of your sins.

Now stop and think about that. Have you ever been star-struck by another person, awed because some individual with an elevated status touched your life in some way? Well, if you are a child of God, you ought to be star-struck by *this* truth: God, the Creator of the heavens and the earth, the Sovereign Ruler of the entire universe and all it contains, called you, justified you, and glorifies you. He guarantees that you are going to live with Him in glory — in heaven forever and ever.

Fifth, God is for you — thoroughly committed to your highest good — no matter what! Look at the question that follows all these facts we've just considered in Romans 8.

What then *shall we say to these things?
If God is for us, who is against us? (v. 31)*

75

Precious child of God — or "want-to-be-and-going-to-be child of God" — the King and Ruler of the universe is for you! No matter what any other human being does to you, no matter what happens to you, no matter what you think or feel or imagine, God is for you.

I want to put it in letters twenty-four feet tall:

GOD IS FOR YOU.

And if God is for you, who can move against you? God is sovereign, and He rules over everything. Whoever has tried to harm you could only go as far as God let them, and not one inch further.

And no matter what they did, no matter how horribly you have been used or abused, God will use it to make you like Jesus. This is His promise.

This life is not the end-all. A glorious, eternal, no-pain, no-sorrow future lies in store for you. As God's child, born into His family, you are going to live forever with the Father, Son, and Holy Spirit.

Sixth, He will take care of you and provide for you. The Bible says, "He who did not spare His own Son, but delivered Him over for us all, how will He not also with Him freely give us all things?" (v. 32).

No matter how deep your hurt right now,

you can make it. If God so loved you that He gave you the ultimate of gifts, the greatest expression of love that He could ever make — which was the life of His Son — will He not also take care of you in every way? Yes, He will. He will provide whatever you need to get through the pain and live as more than a conqueror. And remember He is able; He is omnipotent. Nothing is too difficult for Him. He is God!

Seventh, no hurt is strong enough to separate you from His love. The hurts in our lives can drive us *to* God rather than *from* Him. You may not believe me or be able to handle this right now, but whatever it takes to put you in His arms in total dependence, you will eventually understand was worth it.

Please don't throw this book across the room! Stick with me here.

After you have exhausted every other avenue of relief, you will finally know peace and healing when you lay your head on the chest of your El Shaddai, your All-Sufficient One in faith and rest. Listen to God's Word in Romans 8:35–39:

Who will separate us from the love of Christ? Will tribulation, or distress, or persecution, or famine, or nakedness, or peril, or sword? Just as it is written, "For

Your sake we are being put to death all day long; we were considered as sheep to be slaughtered." But in all these things we overwhelmingly conquer through Him who loved us. For I am convinced that neither death, nor life, nor angels, nor principalities, nor things present, nor things to come, nor powers, nor height, nor depth, nor any other created thing, will be able to separate us from the love of God, which is in Christ Jesus our Lord.

So what do you do with this information as we bring this chapter to a close and before we move on?

May I suggest that you put down this book and find a place to be alone. Clutch a pillow, grab a blanket, and get on your knees (or on your face) on the floor or on the bed and pour out your heart to God.

HEALING TRUTH #5

No hurt is so strong that it can
separate you from His love.
Your hurt is not intended to drive
you from God but to God.

Do it whether He's your Father or not. Tell Him all that is hurting you.

Hurl your questions at Him.

If you are angry, hurt, confused, bitter — whatever — tell Him. If you can't understand why a sovereign God has allowed what He has allowed in your life, tell Him.

Spill out your guts. It's all right to cry, to wail. In fact, many times crying helps release the tension. The Bible talks quite a bit about weeping for sin, for yours or for the sins of others. Why? Because the ultimate source of pain is sin in a universe that God is in the process of redeeming.

Tell God your fears, your frustrations, hurts, disappointments — everything. And when you're finished, ask Him to begin the healing process through His Word. Cry, "Heal me, O LORD, and I will be healed; save me and I will be saved" (Jeremiah 17:14).

Chapter Six:
A Time for Anger

I could see at a glance that this was not a woman who enjoyed her femininity. Not at all.

I had just finished teaching on forgiveness at our singles conference when she came barreling down the center aisle, dressed in a formless gray sweatshirt and jeans. A little roll of fat protruded just below her waist like a small inner tube. Her dark hair hung from her head in greasy strands, creating a stark contrast to the whiteness of her face, without the tiniest bit of makeup on it.

"I can't forgive my father!"

I had never seen nor met the woman before, and yet those were her first words to me, blurted out through taut lips. It was obvious this woman was suffering greatly. Why? I didn't know.

But I intended to find out.

I took her gently by the arm, ushered her to the edge of the platform away from the

80

people, and seated her so that her back would be to the auditorium.

"Now, darlin'," I said, "tell me why you can't forgive your father. What has he done to you?" Like Nehemiah of old, I sent up a silent prayer that God would give me great wisdom and that He would love this woman through me.

"My father got me pregnant and then made me have an abortion," she told me. "Then he got me pregnant again, and this time I had the baby. But my baby was deformed and died. He said that I was a slut, that I had been messing around with boys. But that was a lie. After all that my dad did to me, I didn't want anyone to touch me."

She continued talking, barely pausing for breath.

"Then he got me pregnant *again,* and this time I moved out. My baby was born deformed, but she lived for a year. When she died, I didn't want to live. I tried to kill myself. They put me in a mental hospital and said that I had to have group therapy with my family.

"When I told them what my father did to me, he jumped up, pointed his finger at me, and yelled that I was lying and that I was a no-good slut, just a tramp. My mother jumped up and yelled the same thing at me. So I shut my mouth and didn't say a word for months. I cannot forgive my father."

Her story stopped as abruptly as it had begun. She hadn't looked at me even once since we'd sat down, staring instead at her feet.

My immediate response to this horrible account was, "That makes me so angry."

Her head shot up. "What did you say?"

"What your father did to you," I said. "It makes me *angry*."

"No one has ever said that before," she said, as I reached up to wipe the surging tears off her chin. Her words were so soft, so incredibly tender.

"Oh, darlin', not only does it make me angry, but it makes God angry too. Far more angry. God hates what your father did to you."

These were our first words to each other — words that initiated her healing process. It was a healing that began when she discovered that God also was angry at her father's sin. And that weekend, she made the monumental choice to forgive him.

Three years passed, and in that time God did miraculous things in this woman's life. She now loves being a woman, and you wouldn't recognize her as the same person.

She has lost weight, takes good care of herself, is married, and recently became a mother. She is no longer afraid of her femininity, hiding it for fear it might be violated. She has learned to lean upon God's Word, to trust Him as the Father she never knew. How wonderful it has been to watch God heal her.

How did she heal so rapidly? I think it's because she finally realized that sin makes God very angry. Once she understood this, once her thinking came into alignment with this great truth, she was willing to release her anger to God and forgive her father. She could trust God to judge him appropriately.

When the hurt runs deep, how do we deal with anger, bitterness, and unforgiveness? What does God say about the links in this cruel chain that continuously rub our wound raw, keeping it open and oozing, never healing?

As I write these words, dear reader, I am praying that God will take the truths in this chapter and unlock the chains that have shackled you, so that you might live as more than a conqueror.

WHEN GOD GETS ANGRY

Anger isn't always a sin. There is most certainly such a thing as *righteous anger.* Woe be to us, as a society or as individuals, when sin and injustice no longer provoke anger in our hearts.

As I teach in my book *Lord, Heal My Hurts,* when you do a thorough study of the subject of anger in the Bible, you discover there are more references to God being angry than there are to men being angry. God's righteousness, justice, holiness, and love cannot sit passively by when these attributes are violated. And it doesn't! He expresses Himself in anger — flaring nostrils, heated rage — at such times, and this expression is perfectly right and good.

You can't read the Old Testament or Revelation, the last book of the Bible, without seeing the anger of God or the consequences of His wrath. Sin — disobedience to the revealed Word of God — does not leave God passive. He doesn't shrug His shoulders and say, "Oh well. That's just the way it is." No, His righteousness demands indignation, anger, and wrath at all that goes against His character, at that which violates His commandments and precepts.

The words *anger, angered,* and *angry* are used approximately 364 times in the Old and New Testaments, and as I said, most of these are references to God's anger. Listen to what makes God angry and see if you can relate:

- injustice, idolatry, spiritual adultery, and betrayal[1]
- not listening to what He says[2]
- disobedience, murmuring, and complaining against Him or His servants[3]
- unbelief, and those who suppress truth[4]
- when we refuse to honor Him as God[5]
- when we refuse to listen to His Son[6]
- when we mistreat His people or unjustly touch "the apple of His eye" — Israel,[7] or a child of God

As I mentioned earlier, the Bible makes clear that there will be a "final accounting" on earth for all the evil and hurt people have done to one another. It will be a "day of wrath," when God's anger will be poured out on the ungodly.[8] At that time, they will know and experience the awfulness of their ungodly deeds when God releases His righteous anger on all those who refused to repent or change their minds about their evil.

Why do I say all this?

Because I want to assure you of one very important thing: the ones who have hurt you, abused you, taken advantage of you, and damaged your life will not go unjudged.

HEALING TRUTH #6

Nothing that has ever happened to you
has escaped God's notice. You can
trust that He will bring to account
everyone who has hurt you,
in His time and in His way.

Now, as you think about this, you need to realize that although God feels anger, He is never controlled by it. His anger does not overcome who He is. He has never, ever "lost it," and He never will. God's anger is always kept in balance by His holiness and by all of those attributes that make Him God.

When God expresses anger, then, it is always within the realm of His character, and never contrary to it. It is never unrighteous anger, but rather in perfect harmony with His grace, love, mercy, compassion, and long-suffering. It is always expressed with the intent of ultimate good and justice, and not of evil. Think of what His Word tells us: "For His anger is but for a moment, His favor is for a lifetime; weeping may last for the night, but a shout of joy comes in the morning" (Psalm 30:5).

This truth is repeatedly demonstrated throughout the Word of God. Listen to this good word from Exodus 34:6–7: "The LORD, the LORD God, compassionate and gracious, slow to anger, and abounding in lovingkindness and truth; who keeps loving-kindness for thousands, who forgives iniquity, transgression and sin; yet He will by no means leave the guilty unpunished."

Jesus, the Son of God, felt anger. Remember when He turned over the tables of the money-changers in the temple? Actually, He did it twice, once at the beginning of His public ministry and again at the end.

He was righteously angry, and yet He was righteously controlled — even as He drove them out with a whip! We know from the testimony of Scripture that Jesus always handled His anger in a righteous way, because He always and only did those things that pleased the Father.[9]

BUT WHAT ABOUT *MY* ANGER?

If God's anger is righteous and in perfect keeping with His character, what then can we say about *our* anger? Let me make a few simple observations:

First, anger is a valid emotion, and one that God understands.

Second, while God's anger is always justifiable, ours may or may not be justified.

Third, justifiable or not, we are never to allow anger to *control* us.

When anger takes control of you, watch out! That is the moment when you're in trouble. Galatians 5:16–23 tells us we are to be controlled by the Spirit of God, not by the flesh. And James 1:19–20 lets us know that the wrath of man does not achieve (or bring about) the righteousness of God.

In saying all that, you need to understand that if you don't handle anger in God's way, bitterness will settle in and the hurt will become an ever-present wound. Instead of healing, it will continue to fester. This includes not only anger toward our fellow human beings, but also anger toward God.

As for God, He has no problem at all handling your anger.

The question is, what will that anger do to *you*?

God knows that if you don't deal with the anger, it will turn into a bitterness so vile, so acidic, that it will eat your insides out until you are left a bitter shell of humanity. Have you ever seen that happen to someone? It isn't pretty, is it?

So what do you do if you are angry at God?

Why don't you try *talking* to Him about it?

I suggest that you "Declare and set forth your case," as the Lord said in the book of Isaiah.[10] Talk out your anger with God. Say it aloud or write it out in black and white where you can see it, look at it, and evaluate it.

Then think about all you have learned about Him from the Word of God, or from what I have shared with you to this point in the book. Is your anger with Him justifiable? Has He merited it? Of course the answer is no.

True, you may not be ready to admit that fact. But if you don't, if you continue to hold on to anger against the One who loves you most, then realize this: that anger will become a deadly cancer — a cancer of the soul — that will eventually destroy you. It will rob you of peace, joy, and ministry.

What's the alternative? It's really not rocket science.

Just keep talking to Him.

Pour it all out. Don't stop! Here is Someone who is interested in every word you have to say and has endless patience as you bring to Him all that you've hidden in every nook and cranny of your heart. And when you've said it all, tell Him you recognize that He is God and that because He is, He does not have to answer to you. He can do whatever He pleases. Be contrite; tell Him you are sorry for your prideful rebellion in being angry with Him. Confess your sin.

The fact is, if you have held on to anger against God, you have actually set yourself up as His judge! You have said in your heart that since God is wrong in His dealings with you, then He must also be wrong in His character.

In other words, you (a mere human being who couldn't survive a moment without His granting you breath) have somehow concluded that you know better than God. You've determined what was good and what was evil, what should and shouldn't be, and have sat in the place of God.

My friend, that is pride.

Let that pride be put to shame! Confess that righteousness is found only in Him and that in and of yourself there is no righteousness. As you bow before Him, melt in His arms, submit to Him, and you will find healing. His name is Jehovah Rapha, the Lord God who heals.

Now, what about anger toward others, especially those individuals we think have ruined our lives, wounding us beyond healing?

First of all, is that really true? Can someone damage you beyond healing?

If this is the way you are thinking, then I have wonderful news for you: no human being can ever do anything to you that will ultimately wreck your life. Wound you, yes. Hurt you deeply, yes. Damage you traumatically, leaving mental, emotional, and even physical wounds and scars, sadly yes.

But damage you so you can never be healed? *No.*

I stand by that statement, dear reader, even though psychiatrists, psychologists, and counselors may disagree with me. Why? Because I make my answer on the basis of the character of God and the Word of God.

Think back to the story of Joseph and his comment about his brothers' cruel treatment of him. Do you remember what he said? "As for you, you meant evil against me, *but God meant it for good*" (Genesis 50:20). Joseph clung to what he knew to be true about the character and sovereignty of God — something we also must do when we are angry at those who have harmed us.

Do you remember God's promise in Romans 8:28–31? Let me repeat it for you just in case you don't have it memorized yet. If you will read it aloud three times in a row, three times a day, it will soon be yours.

And we know that God causes all things to work together for good to those who love God, to those who are called according to His purpose. For those whom He foreknew, He also predestined to become conformed to the image of His Son, so that He would be the firstborn among many brethren; and these whom He predestined, He also called; and these whom He called, He also justified; and these whom He justified, He also glorified.

What then shall we say to these things? If God is for us, who is against us?

Because God foreknew you and because He is the Sovereign Ruler of the entire universe, God can orchestrate *every* event in your life in a way that will ultimately be used for His good purpose. And His highest purpose is to make you like His Son, Jesus.

Every event? Yes, e-v-e-r-y event.

Our God is such a magnificent Redeemer! Granted, redemption isn't always seen immediately, and rarely are deep wounds miraculously, instantly healed. In God's time and in His way, however, healing *will* come. It will come right on schedule — His schedule, not ours. Our responsibility is to cling, to trust, to wait, and to believe — to walk in faith one step at a time.

So if you're angry at God, deal with that first. And then, with His help, begin to deal with your pent-up anger toward others. Have you ever seen a television show about some brave individual who deactivates a bomb? That's where we need God's skilled hands, defusing the bomb within us, wire by wire, contact by contact, rendering it harmless.

The alternative, of course, is an explosion, causing untold damage and leaving ruins and debris in its aftermath.

The Bible presents a realistic portrait of human anger, clearly showing us what happens when it takes control of human hearts.

- We see anger seeking revenge.[11]
- We see anger laid up in the heart[12] and left to smolder and burn.[13]
- We see anger stirring up strife.[14]
- We see anger become a raging flood, suddenly gushing out, overwhelming, and covering.[15]

- We see anger bearing grudges and flinging accusations.[16]
- We see anger bringing about sinful actions.[17]
- We see anger that severs friendships.[18]
- We see unreleased anger, held in deep caverns of the heart, that eventually bubbles to the surface as vile, poisonous bitterness. Unchecked, it is a bitterness that will cause trouble and defile many.[19]

If you are to be healed, you must deal with anger and bitterness before they destroy you and those around you.

Is it any wonder then that God tells us in the Word to deal with our anger before the sun goes down? Listen to Ephesians 4:26–27 as you read it aloud:

Be angry, and yet do not sin; do not let the sun go down on your anger, and do not give the devil an opportunity.

"Be angry, and yet do not sin" is a quote taken from Psalm 4:4, which says, "Tremble [with anger], and do not sin; meditate [speak] in your heart upon your bed, and be still. Selah."

Apparently the person pictured in this verse is so filled with anger, so inflamed or burning, that it actually causes him or her to tremble. At times I have been so angry and agitated inside that I was literally shaking. Only I wasn't lying on my bed, as it says in Psalm 4; I was walkin' and talkin'!

So what do you do? Allow the anger to control you? Consume you? Send your blood pressure through the top of your head to the ceiling? No! The One who knows anger knows what to do, and He will instruct you. Listen to Him. Speak truth in your heart, reining in those passions and emotions. Your heart or mind is the command center of your life, and God will give you the strength to make those commands take hold. Tell your heart to be still. Take a deep breath. Let go, relax, cease striving. Calm yourself.

And when do you do this? According to Ephesians 4:26, this is to be done *before* you go to sleep. You must not allow the sun to go down on your anger, because if you do, it will eat into your gut and play havoc with your body.

So how do you do it? Verse 5 of Psalm 4 tells us to "Offer the sacrifices of righteousness, and trust in the LORD."

In other words, you do what is *right,* not what your flesh wants. Put your anger on the altar, slay it, and sacrifice it! Do what

God says is right, and trust Him. God will take care of your situations — all of them — if you will let Him. Don't go to sleep until you settle your anger God's way. Doing so will bring peace to your soul.

Ephesians 4:31 goes on to say this:

Let all bitterness and wrath and anger and clamor and slander be put away from you, along with all malice.

If you don't consciously, willfully put away your anger and bitterness, you will become an angry person. In Proverbs 19:19 God warns us that "A man of great anger will bear the penalty, for if you rescue him, you will only have to do it again."

If you don't deal with anger God's way, the flesh will have *its* way. Listen to the flesh's MO (method of operation):

Now the deeds of the flesh are evident, which are: immorality, impurity, sensuality, idolatry, sorcery, enmities, strife, jealousy, outbursts of anger, disputes, dissensions, factions, envying, drunkenness, carousings, and things like these, of which I forewarn you, just as I have forewarned you, that those who practice such things will not inherit the kingdom of God. (Galatians 5:19–21)

To refuse or neglect to listen to God when He tells you what to do with your anger paints you a fool. "A fool always loses his temper, but a wise man holds it back" (Proverbs 29:11). Ecclesiastes 7:9 says, "Do not be eager in your heart to be angry, for anger resides in the bosom of fools."

Contrast that foolishness with the picture painted in Proverbs 16:32: "He who is slow to anger is better than the mighty, and he who rules his spirit, than he who captures a city." A wise man or woman is one who listens to God and trusts Him to do what He says He will do. In this way, you will be able to let go of your anger and put it into the hands of God. As Paul tells us in the book of Romans: "Never take your own revenge, beloved, but leave room for the wrath of God, for it is written, 'Vengeance is Mine, I will repay,' says the Lord" (Romans 12.19).

Let His nostrils flare — not yours!

If you can grasp and accept the thoughts in this chapter, you will find the chains of anger and bitterness — those rusty iron links that keep our wounds raw and painful — falling off your hands, feet, and heart. These truths will free you from the self-destructive punishment of unforgiveness.

We'll talk about unforgiveness later. For now, let me suggest that before you go any further in the book, you stop and deal with any residual anger lurking in your heart.

How about by tonight, before you close your eyes?

I promise you, you'll rest *so much* better.

Chapter Seven:
At the Root of Your Pain

Who's behind all this hurt that you have suffered or are suffering?

It's the "serpent of old" — the serpent that walked into the Garden of Eden, and slithered out, and who is clearly defined in Revelation, the last book of the Bible, as the devil and Satan.[1] He first appears in Genesis 3 when he seduced the woman with a smooth-as-butter lie and brought death and judgment into our world, as it is to this very day.

Adam and Eve knew there was a tree in the Garden of Eden whose fruit they were not permitted to eat. They also knew the penalty: if they ate it, God warned them, they would die. God had told Adam this fact, and He had made it very clear. When you listen to Eve's response to the serpent's lie, it's also apparent that Eve understood the prohibition very well. She *knew* what God had said.

The woman said to the serpent, "From the fruit of the trees of the garden we may eat; but from the fruit of the tree which is in the middle of the garden, God has said, 'You shall not eat from it or touch it, or you will die.'" (Genesis 3:2–3)

The devil's lie was that she could go ahead and disobey God without consequence. In other words, even though God told her she would die, the serpent claimed she really wouldn't. Instead she would be like God, knowing good and evil for herself. Eve bought the lie. She could decide for herself what was good, what was evil! God was holding out on her!

The very essence of sin is turning to our own way, as Isaiah 53:6 says. So when Adam and Eve ignored God's instructions, followed their own desires, and ate of the forbidden fruit, death entered the world, as Romans 5:12 tells us, through the vehicle of sin. And yes, Adam and Eve truly did die in the course of time, but through all the intervening days before their final physical death, they experienced the fruit of death: separation from God and the pain, hurt, grief, loss, and chaos that come when man plays God.

That, dear friend, is why your hurt runs so agonizingly deep. The ancient root of it goes all the way back to the beginning of man and woman on this earth. Sin is in our very genes as human beings.

In Romans 3, God tells us all have sinned, and the wages of sin is death. The "middle man" of sin and its destructive force, however, is Satan, our adversary. Consider the words of Jesus as He addressed some religious leaders who did not like Him in the least, and who most certainly did not believe He is the Son of God:

"You are of your father the devil, and you want to do the desires of your father. He was a murderer from the beginning, and does not stand in the truth because there is no truth in him. Whenever he speaks a lie, he speaks from his own nature, for he is a liar and the father of lies." (John 8:44)

Job, one of the earliest books of the Bible, gives us critical and invaluable insight into the role Satan plays in our deep personal pain — and the sovereignty of God in it all. In the depths of my own pain, I have found sweet peace of heart as I've read the pages of Job, and I believe the fundamental truths

in this ancient book will help you find hope
and healing for your own hurt.

FROM EARTH TO HEAVEN TO EARTH

The first two chapters of Job serve as a
prologue and setting for the book. As we
look at them, remember what we have
learned thus far about God. Daniel 4:34–35
tells us that God does according to His will
in the army of heaven and among the inhabitants of the earth. Well, that is where
the book of Job takes us in the first chapter.

From earth to heaven to earth.

I could tell you what Job 1 says, but why
should I, when you can read the very words
of God for yourself! As you read, don't miss
how God Himself describes Job. If you've
got that pen or pencil handy, you might
want to circle or color blue everything you
read about Job. Blue is a good color to do it
with, since this is a "true-blue man."

There was a man in the land of Uz
whose name was Job; and that man was
blameless, upright, fearing God and
turning away from evil. Seven sons and
three daughters were born to him.

His possessions also were 7,000 sheep,
3,000 camels, 500 yoke of oxen, 500
female donkeys, and very many servants;

and that man was the greatest of all the men of the east. His sons used to go and hold a feast in the house of each one on his day, and they would send and invite their three sisters to eat and drink with them. When the days of feasting had completed their cycle, Job would send and consecrate them, rising up early in the morning and offering burnt offerings according to the number of them all; for Job said, "Perhaps my sons have sinned and cursed God in their hearts." Thus Job did continually. (Job 1:1–5)

There you have it: a description of a true-blue man of God. He is blameless, upright, fears God, and avoids evil. And if his children happen to slip up, Daddy Job has them covered!

Now, let's leave earth and see what's happening in heaven. Read on. If you have a red pen or pencil, underline the references to Satan — or put a pitchfork over them, as he is so often characterized by that image.

Now there was a day when the sons of God came to present themselves before the LORD, and Satan also came among them. The LORD said to Satan, "From where do you come?" Then Satan answered the LORD and said, "From roaming about on the earth and walking around on it." The LORD said to Satan, "Have you considered My servant Job? For there is no one like him on the earth, a blameless and upright man, fearing God and turning away from evil." Then Satan answered the LORD, "Does Job fear God for nothing? Have You not made a hedge about him and his house and all that he has, on every side? You have blessed the work of his hands, and his possessions have increased in the land. But put forth Your hand now and touch all that he has; he will surely curse You to Your face."

Then the LORD said to Satan, "Behold, all that he has is in your power, only do not put forth your hand on him." So Satan departed from the presence of the LORD. (vv. 6–12)

Satan had been roaming earth and was now back in heaven talking with God. Interesting? *Yes!* Think of what you just learned: Satan has access to heaven, and he and God talk. The book of Revelation gives us even further insight into what takes place during this conversation. We're told that "the accuser of our brethren . . . accuses them before our God day and night" (Revelation 12:10).

Satan knew Job. From what you read, it's apparent the devil had tried to touch Job but couldn't, because God had placed a hedge around His man. God was protecting Job, and Satan couldn't get to him.

Are you thinking, *Lucky Job?* The words came to my mind also, but of course we know it is not luck, but God! There's no such thing as luck if God is sovereign and truly rules over all.

Can you hear Satan's hissing accusation? *"Touch all that he has; he will surely curse You to Your face."* Did you see the gauntlet go down — the glove dropped to the ground, challenging God to a duel?

God didn't miss a beat, did He? He took Satan on. God knew His man and knew that Job would not curse Him . . . or would he? Keep reading, and remember you are reading about something that actually happened. These are God's words, and absolute truth.

Now on the day when his sons and his daughters were eating and drinking wine in their oldest brother's house, a messenger came to Job and said, "The oxen were plowing and the donkeys feeding beside them, and the Sabeans attacked and took them. They also slew the servants with the edge of the sword, and I alone have escaped to tell you." While he was still speaking, another also came and said, "The fire of God fell from heaven and burned up the sheep and the servants and consumed them, and I alone have escaped to tell you." While he was still speaking, another also came and said, "The Chaldeans formed three bands and made a raid on the camels and took them and slew the servants with the edge of the sword, and I alone have escaped to tell you." While he was still speaking, another also came and said, "Your sons and your daughters were eating and drinking wine in their oldest brother's house, and behold, a great wind came from across the wilderness and struck the four corners of the house, and it fell on the young people and they died, and I alone have escaped to tell you." (Job 1:13–19)

Whew! Talk about hurt running deep. Job had lost everything except his wife, his home, and his health.

WHO DID ALL THIS TO JOB?

Who brought such trial and heartache into the life of this good man? Was it God, or Satan?

Satan said to God, "Put forth *Your* hand," and God replied, "Behold, all that he has is in your power, only do not put forth your hand on him." Looks like both were involved, doesn't it? Satan suggested, God permitted, and Satan carried out his plot.

By the way, did you notice the limit God put on Satan: ". . . only do not put forth your hand on him"? Satan couldn't do anything to Job's body. Why? Because, as we have established, God is sovereign and rules over all. It's important that you really grapple with that fact; it will help you as you deal with your own pain.

So who won the duel? Read on —

Then Job arose and tore his robe and shaved his head, and he fell to the ground and worshiped. He said, "Naked I came from my mother's womb, and naked I shall return there. The LORD gave and the LORD has taken away. Blessed be the name of the LORD."

Through all this Job did not sin nor did he blame God. (vv. 20–22)

Tearing the robe and shaving the head were signs of mourning. Under such circumstances, mourning we can understand. But it also says Job worshiped. *Worshiped!* How could Job worship a God who had just allowed such devastation?

Remember now, Job had no idea whatsoever about the conversation between God and Satan. As readers, we understand what's happening here, but only because God wanted it recorded in His book for all the ages. It's the devil, the father of lies, who executed Job's pain. Yet Job attributed it solely to God — and still worshiped Him.

To worship is to bow down, to honor, and to attribute worth. Did you catch Job's words? If not, read them again, out loud. What was Job saying? In essence, he declared, "I had nothing when I came into the world, and I will take nothing with me when I leave. What I have God gave to me, and if He wants, He can take it away."

Job knew God was God and that He had a right to do whatever He pleased. Oh for such faith! What do you suppose would happen with our own hurt if we were to worship God in this way when the hurt comes? Job truly feared God, respecting Him and trusting Him, even in his great shock and sorrow.

Satan, however, wasn't convinced. And so we come to the second chapter of Job. Watch what happens in heaven . . . and then on earth.

ROUND TWO

Again there was a day when the sons of God came to present themselves before the LORD, and Satan also came among them to present himself before the LORD. The LORD said to Satan, "Where have you come from?" Then Satan answered the LORD and said, "From roaming about on the earth and walking around on it." The LORD said to Satan, "Have you considered My servant Job? For there is no one like him on the earth, a blameless and upright man fearing God and turning away from evil. And he still holds fast his integrity, although you incited Me against him to ruin him without cause." (Job 2:1–3)

The evil one had his answer ready; and he was convinced that he would win the battle and alienate this man from his God.

Satan answered the LORD and said, "Skin for skin! Yes, all that a man has he will give for his life. However, put forth Your hand now, and touch his bone and his flesh; he will curse You to Your face." So the LORD said to Satan, "Behold, he is in your power, only spare his life." (vv. 4–6)

Notice once again that God has set limits on what Satan can do to Job. Nothing can touch His man without His permission.

Then Satan went out from the presence of the LORD and smote Job with sore boils from the sole of his foot to the crown of his head. And he took a potsherd to scrape himself while he was sitting among the ashes.
Then his wife said to him, "Do you still hold fast your integrity? Curse God and die!" But he said to her, "You speak as one of the foolish women speaks. Shall we indeed accept good from God and not accept adversity?" (vv. 7–10)

It's an intriguing question, isn't it? "Shall we indeed accept good from God and not accept adversity?" *Shall we?*
Of course if we understand God's sovereignty, we know that we have no choice. And yet those who do not know or do not believe that God is sovereign in heaven and

110

on earth would probably answer "No!" And if we asked why, the majority would probably declare that God is a God of love and He would never permit that. Not their god! (Did you notice the little *g* in god? It's not a typo; rather it reflects that the god of their belief is a little god of their own making, out of their own imagination.)

It is true that God *is* a God of love, but obviously, if we believe the Bible, God *does* permit such things. Maybe those who don't believe a God of love would permit pain into their lives are using a different definition of love than His.

The word for "love" used in relation to God is *agape* or *agapeo* in the Greek. It's a love that desires another's highest good and, therefore, is not occupied with self at all. That's the kind of love God had for Job — and the kind He has for us. In spite of all appearances to the contrary, God truly desired Job's highest good.

We'll explore that in the next chapter as we move further in Job's story, but for now let's consider what we've learned about hurt from Job's experience.

First of all, hurt is not always earned or deserved. It can happen to upright, blameless people. That may be something you need to really get a grip on as you continue to read. It may be that you have suffered so much abuse that you've begun to think there's something seriously wrong with you and that you're somehow getting what you deserve.

But that *wasn't* true for Job, was it?

And it may not be true for you either.

HEALING TRUTH #7

Deep hurt can happen to upright, blameless people; it is not always deserved or earned.

Don't listen to Satan when he comes to you with his smooth, plausible lies, suggesting that you are worthless to God, that you are too flawed to qualify for His love. Remember that he is a liar, a thief, and a murderer. He deceives, divides, and seeks to destroy. Don't let him do that in your relationship with the God who loves you and desires your best!

And don't listen to the thoughts of your mind, the inward voices telling you this isn't true for you. Remember the hiss of the serpent in the Garden of Eden, when he whispered to Eve, "Has God said . . . ?" The devil's strategy is still the same today. He will distort, bend, dilute, or outright deny God's Word.

When He went one-on-one with Satan in the wilderness, Jesus handled the devil's lies simply by quoting the Word of God to him. The same battle tactic works for us today. When we stand firmly on the truths of the Bible, refusing to be deceived or intimidated by our enemy's lies, eventually he will retreat for a while and we'll enjoy a little peace before the next assault.

Here's some encouragement from the apostle James as we close this chapter:

Submit therefore to God. Resist the devil and he will flee from you. Draw near to God and He will draw near to you. (James 4:7–8)

That's more than a pleasant thought. It's a guarantee.

You have God's word on it.

CHAPTER EIGHT:
LIFE CHANGES . . .
GOD DOES NOT

Have you ever experienced a hurt so devastating, demeaning, confusing, unbearable, and inexplicable that you wish you'd never even been born?

Job did.

In the third chapter of Job we read: "Job . . . cursed the day of his birth" (v. 1). He said, "Let the day perish on which I was to be born" (v. 3).

Or maybe you've found yourself looking back on past days that seemed so wonderful, so blessed and happy compared to where you are now. And in reminiscing, you feel even worse about your current circumstances. So much so that you simply wish you were dead.

Do you ever find yourself questioning whether God can truly be trusted? Do you wonder why He allows you to suffer the way you've been suffering? *What have I done to deserve this?* you ask.

Please be comforted with this truth: you are not alone. God has anticipated your questions, and His answer for you is captured in this age-old book of Job.

WITH FRIENDS LIKE THESE . . .

After the book's prologue and the dialogues between God and Satan, the scene shifts to an extended conversation between Job and his friends. It turns out to be a painful discussion because Job's three friends — Eliphaz, Bildad, and Zophar — conclude that Job is suffering so greatly because he has sinned greatly.

Although they are stunned beyond words when they see their old friend's condition, and though they wait seven whole days before saying anything, when they do speak, they let Job have it! They loudly and repeatedly insist that he must have brought the whole mess down on himself. There simply *has* to be sin in his life, or he would never find himself in such a calamitous condition.

As Job listens, the words of these men "torment," "crush," and "insult" him (Job 19:1–3). Instead of helping their grieving friend, the three self-righteous friends only make his sorrows worse and his pain more difficult to bear.

Have you had friends like that?

Ultimately, Job is able to bear it because he knows God's character and His ways. It's a reminder to us that we need to become so firmly established in the Word of God that slanderous attacks and false arguments won't throw us for a loop. We will simply know better. What if Job had believed these three attackers? The story might have ended in quite a different way.

The dialogue continues as Job staunchly defends himself and God. Then when the four of them — Job and the three friends — finally finish talking, a younger man steps into the picture and asks to be heard. Elihu generally refutes the misconception that all suffering is due to sin, as the other men have maintained. Near the beginning of his lengthy discourse, however, Elihu asks Job, "Why do you complain against Him, that He does not give an account of all His doings?" (Job 33:13).

Elihu was right. Job had complained. He had never cursed God, as Satan wanted him to, but at times he seemed to be teetering right on the edge of it. Job simply couldn't understand how or why God had allowed him to end up in such dreadful, heartbreaking circumstances when he'd done everything right.

"I delivered the poor who cried for help,
   And the orphan who had no helper.
The blessing of the one ready to perish
   came upon me,
      And I made the widow's heart sing for
      joy.
I put on righteousness, and it clothed me;
   My justice was like a robe and a turban.
I was eyes to the blind
   And feet to the lame.
I was a father to the needy,
   And I investigated the case which I did
   not know.
I broke the jaws of the wicked
   And snatched the prey from his teeth.
Then I thought, 'I shall die in my nest,
   And I shall multiply my days as the
   sand.' " (Job 29:12–18)

Maybe you have thought something similar about your life. Maybe you imagined that because you chose to do the right thing, your life would always be good and easy and that the path before you would be smooth until the day of your death.

In a broken, fallen world like ours, that simply may not be the case. I think of the multitudes of European Jews in the 1930s and 1940s who had their whole world turned upside down by the Holocaust —

men and women who went from lives of prosperity and fulfillment to the ovens of extermination camps. Such horror defies understanding!

I think of my friend whom I saw just yesterday, and the overnight change in her and her husband's life when their divorced son fell a great distance and was left paralyzed. He now lives with them, his bedroom above theirs. At night she hears Bryan banging on the floor or against the wall because of excruciating pain. Bonnie and I wept together yesterday in prayer. Her home is no longer a "nest," like the one Job spoke about. Life for father, mother, and son all changed with a fall.

I think of forty-year-old David Hames, who was in Haiti, shooting a video on behalf of the relief organization Compassion International when he died in an earthquake, leaving behind a grieving widow and two young sons.

I think of the godly woman whose husband is addicted to painkillers and who has become just a cold shell of the energetic, warm-hearted man she fell in love with. I think of the couple who were preparing to spend their retirement years in overseas ministry — until he was diagnosed with pancreatic cancer and given only weeks to live. I think of the businessman who was highly respected for his analytical abilities and exceptional communication skills, until a tumor wrapped its tentacles through his brain and rendered him nearly incapable of speaking in coherent sentences.

You'll find pain and hurt everywhere if you just ask the right questions and get below the surface of "How are you?" and "I'm fine" polite formalities. Every day, good people suffer excruciating pain. And most often, like Job, we have no satisfying explanation for why such calamity and devastation strikes.

Let's return to Job as he compares his current wretched circumstances with the good old days when he wielded great influence:

"My root is spread out to the waters,
    And dew lies all night on my branch.
My glory is ever new with me,
    And my bow is renewed in my hand.
To me they listened and waited,
    And kept silent for my counsel.
After my words they did not speak again,
    And my speech dropped on them.
They waited for me as for the rain,
    And opened their mouth as for the spring rain.
I smiled on them when they did not

believe,
And the light of my face they did not
cast down.
I chose a way for them and sat as chief,
And dwelt as a king among the troops,
As one who comforted the mourners."
(vv. 19–25)

That's the way things used to be, but this happy picture must have seemed a million miles away to Job after all his suffering. You and I know what happened to that idyllic scene — and how it all began with a dialogue in heaven, a conversation Job knew nothing about. And then . . . suddenly things were very, very different.

Job lost children, possessions, health, and the support of his wife and his friends. In a sense, he was left alone with God . . . *and God was silent.* The greatest man in all the east suddenly found himself without prestige or position. He went from hero to zero. From the most admired man in Uz to the bottom of the heap, the man most to be pitied. Yet from what we read, he was not pitied, but rather disdained and despised.

Satan's game plan was to have Job curse God and die. But if he chose to do that, if he cursed God and turned away from Him, who was left?

Just Satan, the destroyer.
And that's no choice at all.

PAINFUL YEARS

My life is different from Job's in many, many ways.

I've certainly never been as blameless as Job. I've never been as righteous or influential or widely admired. But I can still identify with his hurts and the shock of sudden pain. I have experienced it in my divorce from my first husband and his ultimate suicide. I've experienced it through a tragic death that left a gap in our family circle. And I have experienced it in the hurt of rejection in my own immediate family.

The last four years of my life leading up to the writing of this book have been among the most hurtful I can remember. The events, no longer even in order in my memory, seemed to come one after another after another . . . *an unexpected phone call . . . a trip to the hospital . . . the life of a child hanging in the balance . . . unexpected financial obligations . . . the discovery of a secret, long-buried . . . the death of a dream . . . the news of a violation . . . the rejection of family members who believed a lie . . . the death of one too young to die . . .*

121

the helpless feeling when loved ones refuse to turn to Jehovah Rapha, the God who heals.

On and on it goes. And the hurt seems to plunge into Grand Canyon depths.

What sustains me, my precious husband, and friends who have studied the Word of God with us and walked with us through these dark passages? It is the knowledge that though life changes, God does not.

The book of Job reinforces the truth that you and I are not alone in our suffering. There is nothing new under the sun! Job is thought to be the oldest book in the Bible. He may have been a contemporary of Abraham. And what do we see? We see that our questions about suffering and why God allows it are as old as the oldest stories of man on this earth . . . and the answers are as relevant today as ever.

Earlier in chapter 19, Job responded to Bildad's discourse on the fate of the wicked, justifying himself, saying,

Know then that God has wronged me
  And has closed His net around me. . . .
He breaks me down on every side, and I
  am gone;
  And He has uprooted my hope like a
  tree.

He has also kindled His anger against me
  And considered me as His enemy. . . .
He has removed my brothers far from me,
  And my acquaintances are completely estranged from me.
My relatives have failed,
  And my intimate friends have forgotten me.
Those who live in my house and my maids consider me a stranger.
  I am a foreigner in their sight.
I call to my servant, but he does not answer;
  I have to implore him with my mouth.
My breath is offensive to my wife,
  And I am loathsome to my own brothers.
Even young children despise me;
  I rise up and they speak against me.
All my associates abhor me,
  And those I love have turned against me.
My bone clings to my skin and my flesh,
  And I have escaped only by the skin of my teeth. (vv. 6–20)

And who does Job say has done all this?

Pity me, pity me, O you my friends,
  For the hand of God has struck me.
    (v. 21)

Job attributes his misery to the Lord. You and I know that Satan was involved right from the beginning, yet these events could never have happened unless God gave permission. As we have said repeatedly, God is sovereign. He is supreme over Job's pain and over every circumstance in Job's life.

Blinded as he is by his grief and sorrow, Job hopes for death. Please note, however, that he never once speaks of suicide. That is never an option for this godly man, no matter how deep his suffering. But he does long for death as an escape from his crushing emotional pain.

But then, right in the midst of his near despair, Job has a startling, radiant vision of God as Savior and Redeemer. He makes a declaration of faith that continues to inspire hearts after thousands of years:

As for me, I know that my Redeemer lives,
  And at the last He will take His stand on the earth.
Even after my skin is destroyed,
  Yet from my flesh I shall see God;

Whom I myself shall behold,
  And whom my eyes will see and not
  another. (vv. 25–27)

Job catches a glimpse of the living, change-less God, who would one day enter time and space as a Man, the God-Man, and become the Redeemer for all mankind. It is He who will one day rule the earth as Creator. And suddenly Job is convinced in his heart that he will someday see this One eye to eye.

And what about you, dear reader? Is Jesus your Redeemer? Have you become a new creation by believing in Him and receiving His salvation? Be very sure about this! If there is no change in your life and no power to say no to sin, there is no salvation. The little book of 1 John tells you how you can know for sure. Simply read this short letter near the end of the Bible and mark every occurrence of the word *know.* Then list *what* you know — and how you know it. Then you will *know* if your Christianity is genuine and you are assured of heaven.

In his weakness, Job cursed the day he was born, but he did not curse his God. It would, of course, be a sin to curse God, and that is exactly what Satan wanted to happen . . . so he could prove God wrong about Job.

Would Job do it? Would the strain and pressure eventually push him over that edge? We'll find out together in the next chapter.

CHAPTER NINE: GOD'S ANSWER TO OUR "WHY?"

It didn't feel right, reading that document.

What right had I to read the deposition of a murderer? Nevertheless, I'd been asked to review it, and so I did.

Oh, but it wasn't easy.

It was the murderer's own account of what happened just before he killed a young girl. She had been trying to tell him about Jesus. She told him that what he was doing to her sexually was wrong. It was sin. But she also told him that God could and would forgive him — if he would only believe that Jesus died for his sins. She begged him to be saved.

Instead, he finished his assault and killed her.

I remember dropping the report onto our étagère as I sat on our bed, telling God I just couldn't understand. Why, oh why didn't He intervene? Why did He choose to let this evil go forward? It made me sick at heart. I know God, yes, and I believe He is all that He says He is. But it still made me nauseated to think He would let this evil, twisted man be used by the devil to do unspeakable things to that little girl.

Trying to figure it out in my mind was torment. I couldn't go there. All I could say is, "*Father, I just don't understand this . . . and I'm not going to try. I will trust You. I will rest in what I know about You and cling to that. I will not let my mind go anyplace else. I will not picture the tragedy in my mind. Rather I will think about where that precious little girl is right now — and the sufficiency of Your grace that took her through the atrocity.*

"*You love her more than I do. You held her in Your omnipotent hand and filtered her hurt through Your fingers of love. You are God, and I am a weak, finite human being who cannot even see tomorrow. I don't understand, Father, but I trust You.*"

Admittedly, it is hard to understand why there is such tragedy and suffering in this world — especially in the light of God's sovereignty. If God weren't sovereign, you could blame it all on the devil, demons, man, fate (whatever that is), circumstances, Mother Nature, or whatever forces come to mind.

But if that were true, where would it leave

God? Where would it leave us? Would you really want a God who could be surprised, upstaged, or blindsided by evil powers, sudden storms, violent men, or devastating circumstances? Wouldn't that mean He was overpowered rather than all powerful? Impotent rather than omnipotent? And what would that imply for those of us who trust Him and cling to Him? We would be at the mercy of our circumstances. Driven by the wind. Without hope or consolation.

Have you ever asked God hard questions — questions like Job asked? Have you ever found yourself wondering where He was? Why He didn't rescue you or a loved one? How He could allow such horrific atrocities to take place in our world?

Just within the scope of my own lifetime, I think of men who incarnated terrible evil and killed millions of people or trafficked them as slaves. Men like Stalin, Hitler, Mao Tse-tung, Idi Amin, Pol Pot, and so on. And right here in America, in cities like Atlanta — just two hours away from my front door — young boys and girls are bought, used, abused, and tossed aside by perverted men who refuse to restrain their lusts.

Why does He allow it to happen?

It's a mystery, even to those of us who believe in Him, love Him, and serve Him.

And, beloved, it will *continue* to be a mystery until we see Him face to face. So what do we do? We cling to what we know of God, and we trust and rest in that.

There is a verse in the Old Testament book of Isaiah that I'd like to share with you. It may be one you'd like to memorize. Just read it aloud three times, three times a day, and it will stick — saved in your mind for your heart.

> "That men may know from the rising to
> the setting of the sun
>   that there is no one besides Me.
> I am the LORD and there is no other.
> The One forming light and creating
> darkness,
>   causing well-being and creating calam-
>   ity;
>   I am the LORD who does all these."
>   (Isaiah 45:6–7)

While we're in Isaiah, let me share several other treasures that reaffirm what we're going to see in the final chapters of Job.

> "Remember the former things long past,
>   For I am God, and there is no other;
>   I am God, and there is no one like Me,
> Declaring the end from the beginning,

And from ancient times things which
have not been done,
Saying, 'My purpose will be established,
And I will accomplish all My good
pleasure'; . . .
Truly I have spoken; truly I will bring
it to pass.
I have planned it, surely I will do it."
(46:9–11)

Sufferings and atrocities like those I have
mentioned are impossible to understand.
And yet verses like these lead me to move
forward in trust, as I unite the Word of God
with faith and live in it at that very moment.
In that particular time, in that specific situation, no matter how I feel, I walk in faith's
obedience. It doesn't mean the hurtful,
sometimes incomprehensible mysteries of
life fade away or never bother me anymore;
it just means that when they weigh heavily
on my heart, I have somewhere to turn for
reassurance that God is in control. I have
Someone to whom I can take my questions
and sorrow.

Job poured out his heart, his woes, his
complaints, walking on the ragged edge of
bitterness without stepping over. He questioned God and God's justice. Even though

he fully believed that God is God in all His greatness and majesty, he still couldn't understand why the Almighty One would allow him — a man of integrity and righteous living — to suffer so deeply.

Even so, right down at the bottom line, Job would not deny the character of the Holy One. Though he might not fully understand what God was up to, he was committed to the truth anyway, and would declare it without shame. Remember his bold pronouncement that we read in the previous chapter:

> As for me, I know that my Redeemer lives,
>> And at the last He will take His stand on the earth.
> Even after my skin is destroyed,
>> Yet from my flesh I shall see God;
> Whom I myself shall behold,
>> And whom my eyes will see and not another. (Job 19:25–27)

It's kind of like us as believers, isn't it? We declare what we have heard and learned from the Word of God even when we don't really understand it all. Then something happens: the Spirit of God takes the veil away and our mouths drop open in wonder.

WHEN GOD FINALLY SPEAKS

When Elihu, the fourth and youngest of Job's companions, finished his long discourse — supporting Job in his righteousness, refuting the lie that Job was suffering because of his sin, and noting that God has other purposes in suffering — God finally spoke. Not to the four men but to Job alone.

Before we read this amazing portion of Scripture, take a moment to get away from as many distractions as possible. Turn off the television, radio, and cell phone for a few minutes. If you can, go outside. Read the words slowly, and out loud, picturing the images in your mind's eye. You might want to get that pen or pencil and underline every *you* and *your* that refers to Job, and draw a triangle over every reference to God — or use a yellow highlighter.

Then the LORD answered Job out of the
  whirlwind and said,
"Who is this that darkens counsel
  By words without knowledge?
Now gird up your loins like a man,
  And I will ask you, and you instruct
  Me!
Where were you when I laid the foundation of the earth?
  Tell Me, if you have understanding,

Who set its measurements? Since you
know.
  Or who stretched the line on it?
On what were its bases sunk?
  Or who laid its cornerstone,
When the morning stars sang together
  And all the sons of God shouted for
  joy?

"Or who enclosed the sea with doors
  When, bursting forth, it went out from
  the womb;
When I made a cloud its garment
  And thick darkness its swaddling band,
And I placed boundaries on it
  And set a bolt and doors,
And I said, 'Thus far you shall come,
  but no farther;
  And here shall your proud waves
  stop'?" (Job 38:1–11)

Can you imagine yourself in Job's place,
hearing these words straight from the mouth
of the Lord of the universe? Don't you
imagine he dropped to his knees — and
then to his face? The Lord continued speaking:

"Have you ever in your life commanded
  the morning,

And caused the dawn to know its
place,
That it might take hold of the ends of
the earth,
And the wicked be shaken out of it?
It is changed like clay under the seal;
And they stand forth like a garment.
From the wicked their light is withheld,
And the uplifted arm is broken.

"Have you entered into the springs of
the sea
Or walked in the recesses of the deep?
Have the gates of death been revealed to
you,
Or have you seen the gates of deep
darkness?
Have you understood the expanse of the
earth?
Tell Me, if you know all this.

"Where is the way to the dwelling of
light?
And darkness, where is its place,
That you may take it to its territory
And that you may discern the paths to
its home?
You know, for you were born then,
And the number of your days is great!

Have you entered the storehouses of the
    snow,
    Or have you seen the storehouses of
    the hail,
Which I have reserved for the time of
distress,
    For the day of war and battle?
Where is the way that the light is divided,
    Or the east wind scattered on the
    earth?

"Who has cleft a channel for the flood,
    Or a way for the thunderbolt,
To bring rain on a land without people,
    On a desert without a man in it,
To satisfy the waste and desolate land
    And to make the seeds of grass to
    sprout?
Has the rain a father?
    Or who has begotten the drops of dew?
From whose womb has come the ice?
    And the frost of heaven, who has given
    it birth?
Water becomes hard like stone,
    And the surface of the deep is impris-
    oned." (vv. 12–30)

After speaking about the small things in
nature — blades of grass, crystals of ice,
and drops of dew, the Lord suddenly drew

back the curtain on the expanses of the heavens above and then directed Job's attention to the lion and the raven.

"Can you bind the chains of the Pleiades,
  Or loose the cords of Orion?
Can you lead forth a constellation in its season,
  And guide the Bear with her satellites?
Do you know the ordinances of the heavens,
  Or fix their rule over the earth?
"Can you lift up your voice to the clouds,
  So that an abundance of water will cover you?
Can you send forth lightnings that they may go
  And say to you, 'Here we are'?
Who has put wisdom in the innermost being
  Or given understanding to the mind?
Who can count the clouds by wisdom,
  Or tip the water jars of the heavens,
When the dust hardens into a mass
  And the clods stick together?
"Can you hunt the prey for the lion,
  Or satisfy the appetite of the young lions,

When they crouch in their dens
    And lie in wait in their lair?
Who prepares for the raven its nourish-
    ment
    When its young cry to God
    And wander about without food? (vv.
    31–41)

Let's stop for a moment and consider. What do you observe from marking Job and God? How did Job measure up to Him?

For one more chapter, God continued asking questions about mountain goats, deer, wild donkeys and oxen, ostriches, horses, and hawks. And then He said to Job:

"Will the faultfinder contend with the
    Almighty?
    Let him who reproves God answer it."
    (Job 40:2)

In other words, can a human being — a mere mortal who can't begin to know all that God knows or do all that God does — actually find fault with Him or reprove Him?

And yet, isn't this what we do when we moan, grumble, and complain instead of giving thanks in everything in an act of faith, as we are commanded to do in 1 Thessalonians 5:18?

There is a God, and we aren't Him!

We don't know it all, understand it all, or command it all from the beginning to the end. But God does, and no purpose of His can be thwarted. And so we must answer as Job answered:

"Behold, I am insignificant; what can I reply to You?
I lay my hand on my mouth.
Once I have spoken, and I will not answer;
Even twice, and I will add nothing more." (vv. 4–5)

There is nothing more to say, no argument to be made. We either choose to believe that the sovereign God is in control, or we continue to wallow in misery and rebellion.

GOD AND OUR "WHYS"

I remember sharing the gospel with a woman who turned to me and with flashing bitterness said, "When God gives me back the life of my son, *then* I will believe in Him." What she was saying was that God had done her wrong, and when He undid it, then she would believe.

My only reply was, "Dear one, God gave the life of His only Son for the life of your son — and for you, that you might live together for all eternity."

God's words to Job make it clear that none of us is qualified to call God to account:

> Then the LORD answered Job out of the
>   storm and said,
> "Now gird up your loins like a man;
>   I will ask you, and you instruct Me.
> Will you really annul My judgment?
>   Will you condemn Me that you may
>   be justified?
> Or do you have an arm like God,
>   And can you thunder with a voice like
>   His?" (vv. 6–9)

We can't annul God's judgment. We can't condemn God for not behaving as we think a "good god" should. How absurd to believe — even for a moment — that we could stand in criticism of God! We are human beings.

My friend, which of God's judgments would you change, annul, or undo? Can you even begin to predict all the unforeseen consequences of such an action as they ripple through time?

It's actually a frightening thought, isn't it? Would you really want to put your fingers on God's control board of the universe and start making changes that suit you right now? You and I are mortal, and many times we can't see any further than the end of our noses. Only God is immortal, knowing the end from the beginning.

We may not understand Him or comprehend Him, but we *need* Him!

As Peter once said to Jesus, "Lord, to whom shall we go? You have words of eternal life. We have believed and have come to know that You are the Holy One of God" (John 6:68–69).

> "Who then is he that can stand before Me?
> Who has given to Me that I should repay him?
> Whatever is under the whole heaven is Mine." (Job 41:10b–11)

We are God's. Created by Him and for Him. Created for His pleasure.[1]

The fact is, God isn't required to answer our "whys."

He will answer sometimes. But at other times He simply invites us to trust Him, rest in Him, and wait patiently for Him to guide our thoughts and our ways.

Having seen who He is and knowing He

is all about our redemption, even at the cost of the life of His only begotten Son, should we not join the apostle Paul in saying, "Therefore we also have as our ambition, whether at home or absent, to be pleasing to Him" (2 Corinthians 5:9)?

When we come to the end of our lives, I think we will be very glad if we have simply trusted God and done our best to walk with Him and please Him through all our years. What's the alternative? To turn away from Him? Never! He is our very life! To wallow in helpless anger and bitterness of soul, constantly demanding "Why, why, why?" What a terrible waste of life that would be!

If we could fully understand Him, He would no longer be God.

All of creation is God's! God is not obligated to man, and He didn't have to tell Job (or us) the why of anything — including our suffering.

GOD ISN'T FINISHED
Does Job get it? Listen:

Then Job answered the LORD and said,
"I know that You can do all things,
    And that no purpose of Yours can be thwarted.

142

'Who is this that hides counsel without
   knowledge?'
   Therefore I have declared that which I
      did not understand,
   Things too wonderful for me, which I
      did not know."
'Hear, now, and I will speak;
   I will ask You, and You instruct me.'
I have heard of You by the hearing of the
   ear;
   But now my eye sees You;
Therefore I retract,
   And I repent in dust and ashes." (Job
      42:1–6)

Job's arguments and complaints ceased;
he submitted to the sovereignty of God.
God was under no obligation to give an account of all His doings.[2] Job had seen God
as He really is — "I know that You can do
all things, and that no purpose of Yours can
be thwarted" — and Job changed his mind.
He repented.

As a result, Job passed the test. In spite of
everything, and even in the furnace of great
pressure and pain, Job did not curse God.
And he was the richer for it. The pain that
ran so very deep in Job's life had not been
empty, useless, worthless, wasted. Nor had
it destroyed him. In fact, God worked it into

His perfect plan for this man He loved so deeply.

And He will do the same for you and me, dear reader. Hurt has a distinct purpose in our lives, as we will see in the chapters that follow. But what was its purpose in Job's life — besides giving us an example to learn from?

- Job now knew God in a way he had never known God before.
- Job accepted his hurt as from God, for it was God who permitted Satan to do what he did.
- Job listened to the words of God, and then repented, believed, and obeyed. He gladly laid his own pride in dust and ashes — which is true humility.

But we're still not at the end of the story; God wasn't finished with His servant yet. Remember Job's three friends who frustrated him, mischaracterized him, and were of so little comfort to him in his time of need?

It came about after the LORD had spoken these words to Job, that the LORD said to Eliphaz the Temanite, "My wrath is kindled against you and against your two friends, because you have not spoken of Me what is right as My servant Job has. Now therefore, take for yourselves seven bulls and seven rams, and go to My servant Job, and offer up a burnt offering for yourselves, and My servant Job will pray for you. For I will accept him so that I may not do with you according to your folly, because you have not spoken of Me what is right, as My servant Job has."

So Eliphaz the Temanite and Bildad the Shuhite and Zophar the Naamathite went and did as the LORD told them; and the LORD accepted Job. (vv. 7–9)

When it says the Lord accepted Job, I believe the Bible is speaking of Job's prayer for his friends. This is an important point we don't want to miss: Job was not embittered by his friends' failures, by the pain inflicted on him by their words. Job prayed for his friends. The fact that Job would pray for these men who had treated him so unkindly attests to his walk with the Lord and his desire to act righteously rather than vindictively.

God accepted Job . . . and then pulled out all the stops for him! If you like a book with a happy ending (and who doesn't?), then this certainly fills the bill. Read on:

The LORD restored the fortunes of Job when he prayed for his friends, and the LORD increased all that Job had twofold. Then all his brothers and all his sisters and all who had known him before came to him, and they ate bread with him in his house; and they consoled him and comforted him for all the adversities that the LORD had brought on him. And each one gave him one piece of money, and each a ring of gold.

The LORD blessed the latter days of Job more than his beginning; and he had 14,000 sheep and 6,000 camels and 1,000 yoke of oxen and 1,000 female donkeys. He had seven sons and three daughters. He named the first Jemimah, and the second Keziah, and the third Keren-happuch. In all the land no women were found so fair as Job's daughters; and their father gave them inheritance among their brothers.

After this, Job lived 140 years, and saw his sons and his grandsons, four generations. And Job died, an old man and full of days. (vv. 10–17)

Wow! It is a *wow,* isn't it? How very like

our awesome, loving God!

As I read this heartwarming passage yet again, it seems to parallel what we've seen in Romans 8:28–30. Remember?

> And we know that God causes all things to work together for good to those who love God, to those who are called according to His purpose. For those whom He foreknew, He also predestined to become conformed to the image of His Son, so that He would be the firstborn among many brethren; and these whom He predestined, He also called; and these whom He called, He also justified; and these whom He justified, He also glorified.

In Job's life, God indeed caused "all things to work together for good." And so it is with all who love Him and have been called according to His good purposes.

That doesn't mean that whoever suffers will eventually become wealthy, enjoy long life and health, and have a bunch of children to replace the ones who died. Rather, I believe, God is showing us that the end is better — *we* are better — because of the suffering.

We'll explore that subject more a little

later. For now, just remember the end of every child of God is *glory:* glorious, beautiful, radiant eternal life in the presence of God, and the end of all our sorrow, pain, tears, and death.

There is no greater work on suffering and the why of suffering than the book of Job. It's a divine masterpiece, God's word to us when our suffering is not the consequence of sin. It is His answer to our "Why?" He is God, and we must trust Him. Why?

The writer of Hebrews tells us that "without faith it is impossible to please Him, for he who comes to God must believe that He is and that He is a rewarder of those who seek Him" (11:6). So what can you do with these truths when the hurt runs deep?

- *Worship God* — even in the midst of your pain. Bow before Him, trust Him. Listen to what Job said: "But it is still my consolation, and I rejoice in unsparing pain, that I have not denied the words of the Holy One" (Job 6:10).

- *Remember that Satan plots to use suffering to entice you into sin* — and the primary sin in anyone's life is unbelief. Your adversary will do all that he can to create unbelief in your heart, seeking to persuade you that God won't

148

do what He said, that He'll somehow hold out on you or keep His best from you. Satan's ultimate aim, just as with Job, is to get you to curse God and turn your back on Him. Don't be taken in by the devil's lies! The truth is that whatever comes into your life is filtered through God's sovereign fingers of love.

- *Be assured that whatever you endure is not more than you can bear.* Memorize 1 Corinthians 10:13: "No temptation [can also be translated *trial* or *testing*] has overtaken you but such as is common to man; and God is faithful, who will not allow you to be tempted [*tried* or *tested*] beyond what you are able, but with the temptation [*trial* or *testing*] will provide the way of escape also, so that you will be able to endure it." I can't tell you how many times God has brought this verse to mind and how it has helped me through a difficult moment.

- *Know that your pain is not in vain.* The hurt that ran deep in Job's life was not empty, useless, worthless, wasted hurt; it brought him and his friends to a new and deeper understanding of God. If God has touched your heart through

Job's hurt, know this: He will touch the hearts of others through yours if you respond properly. Our great Redeemer will redeem your pain as He uses your story and victory in the lives of others.

I'll never forget sitting and talking with Ruth Graham, and the comfort that I gained in knowing that she and Billy also had a rebellious son, Franklin.

And now? He proclaims the gospel of Jesus Christ around the world for the Billy Graham Evangelistic Association. Since 1989, he has preached to more than three million people in 126 evangelistic events. He also heads up Samaritan's Purse, a prominent international Christian relief organization, bringing hope and help to suffering and disadvantaged people in over one hundred nations of the world.

It's just another reminder that when we serve an all-loving, all-powerful God, we have no idea of the good He can weave from the tangled, broken, and frayed threads of our lives.

CHAPTER TEN:
SUFFERING WE
BRING ON OURSELVES

Life for Debbi as a little girl seemed wonderfully normal. She played with dolls and friends and dreamed of growing up and meeting Prince Charming. She was part of a family of four, including Mom, Dad, and an older brother.

No, God wasn't in their lives. Since Debbi's family never went to church, she didn't know enough about God to even miss Him.

Debbi's parents had quarreled and squabbled for as long as she could remember, but as she headed into puberty, it became much worse. Through all the anger and shouting and insults, Debbi wondered if her parents really loved her — or if anyone loved her.

At thirteen, Debbi's little-girl world changed forever. She became pregnant. Here's her account of those devastating changes.

I'll never forget riding in the backseat of my mother's car on the way to the abortion clinic. When I looked in the rearview mirror I saw the hatred in her eyes as she drove me to the clinic where they would end my pregnancy. This was not the first time I felt that my mother hated me. She told me she wished I was never born at other times.

Soon after the abortion I started feeling completely worthless. I started hurting myself in various ways to get "attention," like setting the shoes that I was wearing on fire and sipping rubbing alcohol. I had let down my mother and myself. These feelings got so strong I had wanted to end my life, and I made my first serious suicide attempt. I took over a hundred antidepressants and went into a coma. Two and a half days later by a miracle of God I woke up and recovered completely.

At sixteen . . . I started drinking and doing drugs a lot just to numb the pain. My life seemed out of control, and with a new boyfriend came another pregnancy and another abortion. During my first abortion I had been put to sleep, but during this one I was fully awake and realized that what I was doing was murder. It was one of the loneliest times of my life.

Not long after this I attempted suicide again by jumping from my boyfriend's truck that was going over fifty-five miles per hour. I landed in a ditch, injured and bleeding, and he just drove away.

Debbi's e-mail went on for pages and pages, as she described a life that spiraled down and down into the worst human sewer you can imagine.

But gloriously, God did not leave her in the hole she'd dug for herself. Through His great grace and kindness, she eventually found forgiveness and new life in Jesus Christ. She is now married with a husband and family and her own beauty salon. And God is restoring her inwardly as well, bringing to mind how God can give us beauty for ashes.[1]

Pain of Your Own Making

We saw in Job's story that devastating pain can come into a person's life through no fault of their own. But what do you do when a lot of the hurt is of your own making?

Because you broke God's law.

Because you refused to turn to Him.

Because you were determined to go your

own way.

Granted, you may have had only the vaguest notion of His existence. But did you know — deep down — that drugs, alcohol, stealing, cheating, lying, sex outside of marriage, and rebellion against authority were wrong? What about those "smaller," more ordinary things, like . . . speaking damaging words to your family, or hiding credit card charges from your spouse, or sharing secrets that weren't yours to share — all leading to the pain of ruptured relationships?

Most likely you knew, at some level, that what you were doing was wrong.

But you went ahead anyway.

If you attempted to justify some of these things on the basis of "It's not my fault; look at what's been done to me," you knew in your heart of hearts that sort of thing wouldn't wash. You knew you were in the wrong. Yes, you may have acted out of disappointment, abandonment, or emotional pain. But what about those who have had those same life issues — or worse — yet chose not to take the path of destruction and death?

Sin is sin, and with it comes built-in consequences. James wrote, "Then when lust has conceived, it gives birth to sin; and when sin is accomplished, it brings forth

154

death" (1:15). Death in some form always follows sin. It may be the death of innocence, childhood as it should be, purity, relationships, marriage, health, or opportunities to serve God and advance His kingdom.

The purpose of this chapter is not to beat you up about the wrong choices in your past, if that happens to be your situation. Far be it from me! You have your hands full with emotional pain as it is.

Here's what I hope to get across in this chapter: when we do what is right in our own eyes but not in God's, we will find ourselves facing a set of consequences. But God has no desire to leave us stewing in the juices of our own sinful choices. When we submit to Him and seek His help, we can get through those consequences and step onto the path to hope and healing.

HEALING TRUTH #8

When we sin, we will find ourselves facing the consequences. But when we submit to God in repentance and seek His help, we can get through those consequences and step onto the path to hope and healing.

That's what God's Word teaches, and the more we understand that teaching, the better it will be for us.

A study of the Old Testament prophets makes it clear that the suffering of God's people, Israel, was of their own doing. They disregarded God's direction, broke God's commandments, fell down to worship false and despicable idols, turned to other nations for help instead of to God, and refused to listen to Him speak through His messengers and prophets. Listen to His words through Jeremiah:

> "A voice is heard on the bare heights,
>   the weeping and the supplications of
>   the sons of Israel;
>   because they have perverted their way,
>   they have forgotten the LORD their
>   God." (3:21)

They had perverted their way and forgotten God. And yet what did God say to them?

> "Return, O faithless sons, I will heal your faithlessness." (v. 22)

And what would God say to us today? Take a good look at the United States of America and you will see much the same in our nation as a whole. Like Israel of old, we have perverted our way and forgotten the Lord our God. This is why the hurt runs so destructively deep in our families and society in general. We think we can put God on the side burner and let Him steam a little, while we turn each one to our own way.

You can't do that to God. It brings destruction. Look at what is happening in our nation today. We are reaping the harvest of our sins. God's kettle is about to go dry.

"Why do you cry out over your injury?
Your pain is incurable.
Because your iniquity is great
And your sins are numerous,
I have done these things to you."
(Jeremiah 30:15)

And yet the affliction comes that we might turn to Him and cry for healing.

O LORD, the hope of Israel,
All who forsake You will be put to shame.
Those who turn away on earth will be written down,
Because they have forsaken the fountain of living water, even the LORD.
Heal me, O LORD, and I will be healed;

157

Save me and I will be saved,
For You are my praise. (Jeremiah
17:13–14)

When you look at the calamity that man
has brought upon himself, the awful consequences of sin and rebellion, surely you
understand the longings within the prophet's aching heart. I know they have been the
cry of my own heart.

For the brokenness of the daughter of
my people I am broken;
I mourn, dismay has taken hold of me.
Is there no balm in Gilead?
Is there no physician there?
Why then has not the health of the
daughter of my people been restored?
(Jeremiah 8:21–22)

There *is* healing, beloved, but only according to God's precepts. Like Job, those who
wish to be healed must listen to God. They
must say to Him as Job did, "I will ask You,
and You instruct me" (Job 42:4).

But just in case you're still wondering if
you or someone you know has gone too far
and is now out of God's reach or care, I'd
like to introduce you to someone. In fact,
he was a king over the nation of Judah, in
the Old Testament. But just because he was

king over God's people didn't mean he was God's man.

Far, far from it.

THE WORST OF THE WORST

Manasseh was of the tribe of Judah and the house of David. He became king when he was twelve and reigned for fifty-five years, from 697 to 642 BC.

His father, Hezekiah, had been a godly man.

In that sense, the apple couldn't have fallen further from the tree; Manasseh, Hezekiah's son, was thoroughly evil.

In fact, when it comes to kings, there was none worse.

Because of his position of great responsibility and power, with the awesome privilege of sitting on David's throne, Manasseh's sin was no private matter. It had a devastating impact on others.

Most sin, whether or not we realize it or admit it, hurts and damages others. In many ways, sin is like a deadly virus; unchecked, it spreads, infecting many, many lives. The Bible tells us that Manasseh seduced God's people "to do more evil than the nations whom the LORD destroyed before the sons of Israel" (2 Chronicles 33:9).

The nations being referred to are those

159

God had ordered Joshua to destroy when Israel moved into Canaan, the land God had sworn by covenant to give to Abraham and his descendents as an everlasting possession when the iniquity of the Amorites was full.[2] The land — covering far more territory than the modern nation of Israel has now — was to belong to Israel forever. And so it will be in a time to come. Our sovereign God has said so!

Years after God had destroyed those nations for their sin, His own chosen people were described as being even more evil.

Manasseh . . .

. . . made Judah sin with his idols,

. . . built altars for them and for all the "host of heaven" in the temple that was erected for the worship of God alone,

. . . sacrificed his own sons in the fire as part of that worship,

. . . practiced witchcraft,

. . . put an image of Asherah, a female god, in the house of the Lord, and

. . . filled Jerusalem from one end to the other with innocent blood.[3]

You would certainly expect God's righteous judgment to fall on this man, and that's exactly what happened. But first, note how God called to Manasseh and gave him the opportunity to repent and turn around.

What grace! The evil king, however, would have none of it. He left God no choice but to let judgment fall.

> The LORD spoke to Manasseh and his people, but they paid no attention. Therefore the LORD brought the commanders of the army of the king of Assyria against them, and they captured Manasseh with hooks, bound him with bronze chains and took him to Babylon. (vv. 10–11)

The hooks went into his nose, the shackles and chains went around his arms and legs, and he was marched off to faraway Babylon — present-day Iraq.

So that was that, right? Manasseh got what was coming to him, end of story, right?

Certainly Manasseh would have rotted in his chains in a Babylonian dungeon if he hadn't done something he had probably never done before.

He called out to God.

And he really meant it.

> When he was in distress, he entreated the LORD his God and humbled himself greatly before the God of his fathers. (v. 12)

161

Job had humbled himself too, but Manasseh was no Job! There was no contest by Satan to get Manasseh to curse God; his whole life had cursed Him. Yet when Manasseh humbled himself, God responded.

When he prayed to Him, He was moved by his entreaty and heard his supplication, and brought him again to Jerusalem to his kingdom. Then Manasseh knew that the LORD was God. (v. 13)

Isn't that something? Job cried out to God, and finally God spoke in reply, helping Job to know Him as he never had known Him before. And Manasseh, in his turn, saw that the Lord was God when God was moved by his prayer for mercy.

The shocking result — are you ready for this? — is that sovereign God allowed Manasseh to go back to Jerusalem, live productively, at least begin to clean up his mess, and order Judah to serve the Lord! Listen . . .

Now after this he built the outer wall of the city of David on the west side of Gihon, in the valley, even to the entrance of the Fish Gate; and he encircled the Ophel with it and made it very high.

162

Then he put army commanders in all the fortified cities of Judah. He also removed the foreign gods and the idol from the house of the LORD, as well as all the altars which he had built on the mountain of the house of the LORD and in Jerusalem, and he threw them outside the city. He set up the altar of the LORD and sacrificed peace offerings and thank offerings on it; and he ordered Judah to serve the LORD God of Israel. Nevertheless the people still sacrificed in the high places, although only to the LORD their God. (vv. 14–17)

Yes, there was great residual damage from Manasseh's sin, and we can expect the same from ours. I still live with some consequences in my own life, but I handle them in faith. The fact is, each of us is accountable for our choices. Our parents, or others who could have served as faithful role models, might not have been or done what they should have, but we can't hold them guilty for *our* behavior.

We might try to point the finger of blame elsewhere, but it won't work. Those who harmed us cannot be our excuse for sin or rebellion. Our response to pain, hurt, and suffering is *our* decision, and each of us is accountable for our own sins. (One dear woman shared with me that her psychologist taught her to blame her mother, but it didn't resolve her hurt. Of course it didn't!)

HEALING BEGINS WITH CONFESSION

If we are going to experience authentic healing in our lives, then we must accept accountability for our actions against God and against truth. Excusing our actions is as useless as sweeping dirt under a rug. The filth continues to filter into the crevices of our lives. True and lasting healing comes only when our sin is exposed to the light of God's holy, cleansing truth.

One of the saddest stories in all the Bible describes how King David, a man greatly beloved of God, fell into sin and committed adultery with Bathsheba, the wife of one of his most valiant soldiers. That would have been bad enough! But when the king discovered that Bathsheba was pregnant from their union, he arranged for her husband to be placed in a dangerous situation in battle, where he would inevitably be killed.

For some time, King David tried to cover up his sin and guilt — until God called his hand through fearless Nathan the prophet. Finally comprehending and admitting the depth of his sin, David humbled himself, repented, and returned to the Lord.

As he looked back on that whole epoch in his life — the evil of his actions, the self-inflicted wounds, and the grace of God — David wrote Psalm 51. It is a marvelous testimony to all of us who hurt because we didn't fear God, respect Him, or trust Him as we should. Listen to David's agonizing, heartfelt prayer. Then if you want God to heal the hurt you brought upon yourself through your sin, make it *your* prayer.

Be gracious to me, O God, according to
  Your lovingkindness;
    According to the greatness of Your
    compassion blot out my transgressions.
Wash me thoroughly from my iniquity
  And cleanse me from my sin.
For I know my transgressions,
  And my sin is ever before me.
Against You, You only, I have sinned
  And done what is evil in Your sight,
  So that You are justified when You
  speak
  And blameless when You judge.

Behold, I was brought forth in iniquity,
  And in sin my mother conceived me.
Behold, You desire truth in the inner-

most being,
And in the hidden part You will make
me know wisdom.
Purify me with hyssop, and I shall be
clean;
Wash me, and I shall be whiter than
snow.
Make me to hear joy and gladness,
Let the bones which You have broken
rejoice.
Hide Your face from my sins
And blot out all my iniquities.

Create in me a clean heart, O God,
And renew a steadfast spirit within me.
Do not cast me away from Your pres-
ence
And do not take Your Holy Spirit from
me.
Restore to me the joy of Your salvation
And sustain me with a willing spirit.
Then I will teach transgressors Your
ways,
And sinners will be converted to You.

Deliver me from bloodguiltiness, O
God, the God of my salvation;
Then my tongue will joyfully sing of
Your righteousness.
O Lord, open my lips,

That my mouth may declare Your
  praise.
For You do not delight in sacrifice,
  otherwise I would give it;
  You are not pleased with burnt offer-
  ing.
The sacrifices of God are a broken spirit;
  A broken and a contrite heart, O God,
  You will not despise. (vv. 1–17)

In 1 John 1:9–10 God assures us that
when we confess our sins — naming them
and owning up to them before God — God
is faithful and righteous to forgive our sins
and to cleanse us from all unrighteousness.
By contrast, if we say that we have not
sinned, we make Him a liar and His word is
not in us.

As much as you might wish you could,
you cannot cover your sin. To *not* agree with
God that sin is sin, to not hold God's
viewpoint on sin or to try to twist it to ac-
commodate your sins is to say that God has
lied. You must recognize and deal with your
sin. When you do that, then God not only
forgives your sin, He cleanses you from all
sin. Why? Because He knows your heart to
be right with Him.

The bottom line, dear reader?
You must call sin *sin*.

King David did that and found forgiveness and restoration. The same can be true for you.

Now, will confession and forgiveness bring back the baby you aborted? Will it erase the damage your sins have caused in the lives of others? No, it won't.

Will it restore to you what you wasted, mishandled, or destroyed? Perhaps, but not necessarily.

Will you endure sorrow for the rest of your days on earth? We will discuss that in the next chapter.

What confession *will* do is start the process of healing in your heart. It will set you on the path toward hope because you will know without a doubt that you are walking in relationship with God. Proverbs 28:13 says, "He who conceals his transgressions will not prosper, but he who confesses and forsakes them will find compassion."

Before you go any further, what do you need to do about your sin? Do what David did! Acknowledge it, don't bury it. Confess it. Write out your own psalm to the Lord. Or sit quietly and pour out your soul before Him.

God hears the cries of mankind. He heard Job's, He heard Manasseh's, He heard David's, and He will certainly hear yours as well.

His office hours are twenty-four hours a day, seven days a week. In fact, He's waiting for you right now.

CHAPTER ELEVEN:
HAS HOPE FADED FOREVER?

Atlanta, the lovely historical city of the Old South, blossoms into a wonderland of beauty in the spring. White dogwoods are so profuse and airy, it seems God has sprinkled "baby's breath" across the lawns of stately old neighborhoods, amongst the rich pink and red blooms of grand azaleas that have been there as long as the magnificent homes they adorn.

On a sunny morning in May, the northwest section of this city will take your breath away.

Behind all the flowers and charming old neighborhoods, however, the city known as "the capital of the South" hides a dark and terrible underbelly.

This is a city where 129 girls are raped ten to fifteen times a day — and on Thursdays through Saturdays, every fifty-four seconds a girl is raped through forced prostitution.[1] It's a city with more strip clubs than Las Vegas, and it's one of the top three cities in the United States for child prostitution.

Think of how many walk the streets of this once-genteel southern city in tears because of the sin of the city!

Opening the Old Testament book of Lamentations, we see another urban scene — a once-proud city devastated by war and filled with tears of sorrow and regret. The people are despised and in mourning.

The city is Jerusalem in the days following its defeat and destruction at the hands of the Babylonian army. The once-lovely temple of the Lord has been thrown down to its foundation and burned. Many of Jerusalem's citizens have been slain, their corpses left where they fell; others have been marched off as slaves to Babylon. The dazed survivors, not even fit for the march to Babylon, now sit mourning on the streets, with nothing left but their memories.[2]

Why would a sovereign God allow the fierce, impetuous, ruthless, idolatrous Babylonians such a victory? Why would He not defend His people, the city where He put His name and His temple?

The prophet Jeremiah, one of those left behind and in all probability the author of the book of Lamentations, wrote: "Jerusalem sinned greatly. . . . Her uncleanness was in her skirts; she did not consider her future. Therefore she has fallen astonishingly" (Lamentations 1:8–9).

You dabble in sin, and you don't realize you're in quicksand.

You sin, but you don't consider your future.

"She did not consider her future. Therefore she has fallen astonishingly." It's quite a statement to ponder, isn't it?

Therefore is a term of conclusion. In other words, sin carries a consequence.

In the first chapter of the New Testament book of James, God makes it clear that when lust conceives — when our desires rule and have their satisfaction — a child is born: Sin. And Sin, in turn, brings forth Death.[3]

Death had come to Jerusalem. Here's how Jeremiah described the extent of the city's destruction: "Your ruin is as vast as the sea; who can heal you?" (Lamentations 2:13).

Do you feel that way? Can you understand or sympathize — because you feel ruined, or you look at those you love and grieve over how they have ruined their lives? They didn't stay away from sin, and when you found out, you sounded the alarm, but they wouldn't listen.

HAS HOPE FADED FOREVER?

Many so-called prophets in Jeremiah's day were not truly men of God. As it is today, plenty of charlatans were masquerading as spokesmen and spokeswomen for God. They were popular too. Why? Because people wanted to hear things that made them feel good, not truths that exposed their sin. They wanted assurance that God would never bring judgment on His people and His holy city. So the prophets gave the people the false and foolish visions they wanted. They didn't expose their sin so they could be restored from captivity.[4]

As a result, they sank deeper into sin — and into the inevitable hurt, pain, and destruction.

A just and righteous God did "what He has purposed; He has accomplished His word which He commanded from days of old. He has thrown down without sparing, and He has caused the enemy to rejoice over you; He has exalted the might of your adversaries" (v 17).

I have a mental picture of walking through the ruined city at night, the stench of death and burning still heavy in the air, and hearing the cries and moans of the survivors.

Is all lost? Has hope faded forever? "Is there no balm in Gilead? Is there no physician there?" (Jeremiah 8:22).

What about in your own life? As you look at the destruction, at the dreams and desires razed by sin — whether your sin or someone else's — is there any reason to hope for restoration?

Yes, there is hope because God is! He exists, and He's a God of hope. Even if the hurt was of your own making, dear one, God remains God. He is the Redeemer. Redemption is His business.

Listen to Jesus' own mission statement for Himself: "The Son of Man did not come to be served, but to serve, and to give His life a ransom for many" (Mark 10:45). He came to buy you out of the slave market of sin and to set you free so you could be sold no more![5]

But let's return to Lamentations:

Remember my affliction and my wandering, the wormwood and bitterness.
Surely my soul remembers
And is bowed down within me. (3:19–20)

It's really easy to remember our failures, isn't it? We might forget everything else — our address, our phone number, our shopping list, our PIN numbers — but our failures dance before our eyes in Blu-ray high-definition detail and living color! That's because Satan, the accuser and enemy of our soul, loves to bring them to our remembrance. Why? Because he hates us and would love nothing better than to discourage and defeat us, leading us into depression and despair.

So what are we to do? Are we to continue staring at our failures? Rehearsing them over and over? Wondering what possessed us to do what we did? Thinking, *If only I had made another choice that day, that night . . .*

Will that help or make the bad memories fade? No. In fact, we likely will find ourselves sinking deeper, from discouragement into despair.

So what do we do with our past failures and regret? We look away from them, turn our focus to God, and remember this instead:

This I recall to my mind,
   Therefore I have hope.
The LORD's lovingkindnesses indeed
   never cease,
   For His compassions never fail.
They are new every morning;
   Great is Your faithfulness.
"The LORD is my portion," says my soul,

"Therefore I have hope in Him."
(Lamentations 3:21–24)

"Therefore I have hope. . . . Therefore I have hope in Him."

Why? Because God is who He is and because He never changes but is the same yesterday, today, and forever.

HEALING TRUTH #9

Wherever you are, whoever you are, whatever you have done, there is hope because there is God. He is a God of hope; redemption is His business.

Wherever you are, whoever you are, whatever you have done, there is hope because there is God. Even if you are in a pit that you dug with your own hands.

Remember King Manasseh and King David, men we read about in the previous chapter, and how they were restored? Even the desperately wicked King Ahab was heard when he cried to God.[6] Countless stories could be told, from the annals of history, from the four corners of the earth, from the lives of multitudes today, of God's great deliverance of the greatest of sinners.

For myself, I stand in awe of God — to

think that He would choose to bring me to Himself when I had turned my back on Him. He brought me to my knees in utter desperation when I could not break the bonds of sin. And now, by His grace, here I am writing a book to tell you and others what to do when the hurt runs deep.

Sometimes when I stop to think about it, it staggers my mind. Defies my reason. Who am I? Nothing. Nobody. Naturally unqualified for what I do, *but God . . . !* He has redeemed my life from the pit that I dug with my own hands, the pit I sunk into so deeply.

Why do such sinners find such mercy? How can the worst get rescued when they deserve the just judgment of God?

The apostle Paul referred to himself as the worst of sinners (see 1 Timothy 1:15). And yet because of God's more than abundant grace, this blasphemer and persecutor found faith and love in Christ Jesus.

Let's let Paul explain it, as he does so well under the inspiration of the Almighty:

Yet for this reason I found mercy, so that in me as the foremost [of sinners], Jesus Christ might demonstrate His perfect patience as an example for those who would believe in Him for eternal life. (v. 16)

As you might imagine, Paul felt overwhelmed by such grace, mercy, and kindness. He could only exclaim words of praise: "Now to the King eternal, immortal, invisible, the only God, be honor and glory forever and ever. Amen" (v. 17).

And that's how I respond too.

God reminds His people — both Israel *and* us — that "The Lord will not reject forever, for if He causes grief, then He will have compassion according to His abundant lovingkindness" (Lamentations 3:31–32).

Did you read those words carefully? Oh, please do. These are words from the very mouth of God Almighty. It is the character of God, not the character of man, that rescues and restores the sinner. If you will remember this and act accordingly event by event, incident by incident, thought by thought, throughout the remaining days of your life, resting in who God is, you will find yourself able to live through the hurt — above the hurt — as more than a conqueror.

Oh, beloved, please listen to me. Everything in life rests on God. Your responsibility is to rest in Him. That's what it means

178

to live by faith. And the sooner you begin to practice this life of rest, moment by moment, memory by memory, bringing every thought captive to the obedience of faith,[7] the more glorious your life will be — even in the presence of hurtful and difficult circumstances.

Yes, it's inevitable that we will experience seasons of grief and sorrow over sin and its consequences, but there comes a time to put away the laments, the mourning. If you don't learn how to resolve your sorrow and deal with your pain, depression will become your enemy, lurking at your door.

Let the Lord lift you up. Let your mourning be turned to dancing. Listen to what God had David write in Psalm 30:

I will extol You, O LORD, for You have
  lifted me up,
    And have not let my enemies rejoice
    over me.
O LORD my God,
  I cried to You for help, and You healed
  me.
O LORD, You have brought up my soul
from Sheol;
  You have kept me alive, that I would
  not go down to the pit.

Sing praise to the LORD, you His godly
ones,
   And give thanks to His holy name.
For His anger is but for a moment,
   His favor is for a lifetime;
   Weeping may last for the night,
   But a shout of joy comes in the morn-
   ing. . . .

You have turned for me my mourning
into dancing;
   You have loosed my sackcloth and
   girded me with gladness,
That my soul may sing praise to You and
not be silent.
   O LORD my God, I will give thanks to
   You forever. (vv. 1–5, 11–12)

The past is past. As Paul counsels us in
Philippians 3:13, we're to forget those
things which are behind us. Refuse to let
your mind go there. Rein in your thoughts.
There is nothing you can do to change what
has already happened. So why waste your
time and energy and exacerbate the pain?
   Instead, sing to the Lord. Sing a new song
to Him! Move forward, remembering that
you serve a sovereign, omnipotent God, who
tells us that nothing is too difficult for Him.

You, O LORD, rule forever. . . .
Restore us to You, O LORD, that we may
be restored. (Lamentations 5:19–21)

CHAPTER TWELVE: WALKING THROUGH THE FIRE . . . BUT NOT ALONE!

God will not abandon you.

Nor must you abandon God.

If you are a child of God, no matter whether your suffering has come about through your own sins and failure or not, you can rest assured that He will never turn away from you.

You may *feel* alone and abandoned at times, but you are not.

There are two verses from the Bible I want to strongly urge you to learn by heart. They were written to Christians who were in the midst of suffering.

The government didn't like their Christianity. It was an offense to their society.

They were accused of all sorts of hate crimes. They were made public spectacles, treated shamefully.

Some ended up in prison.

Others identified with those who were imprisoned — and reaped the consequences.

Some lost everything, all their material possessions.

Marriages were tried, attacked relentlessly by the temptations of a society torn away from its moral moorings.

Money became an issue, as opportunities to earn a living among those who resented and rejected them were ruthlessly cut off.

Their faith was severely tested. Would God really provide? Would they be content with what He provided?

And in the midst of so much hurt and suffering, the writer of Hebrews reminded them that God had given them these strong words to hold on to:

I will never desert you, nor will I ever forsake you. (Hebrews 13:5)

(The original Greek has five *never/evers* for emphasis!)

He told them this so they could confidently reply:

The LORD is my helper, I will not be afraid. What will man do to me? (v. 6)

Their helper — our helper — is Jesus Christ, who is the same yesterday and today and forever.[1] Jesus, who was made for a little while lower than the angels and became man, was the one who suffered death for us. He was the one who suffered reproach outside the city on a cross — the most wretched and ignominious of deaths, as the author of Hebrews reminds us in verses 12 and 13:

Therefore Jesus also, that He might sanctify the people through His own blood, suffered outside the gate. So, let us go out to Him outside the camp, bearing His reproach.

In light of this truth, those who place their trust in Him are not to shrink back in shame, give up, or consider ourselves in any sense abandoned by God. Nor are we to abandon our faith and our integrity. Rather, we are to go to Him, outside the camp, bearing His reproach.

Did you notice the charge to "go out to Him," to be with Him and share in His suffering? This is what Christianity is all about: denying ourselves, following Him. It is the "fellowship of His sufferings," as Philippians 3:10 says. This is what you must remember when the hurt runs deep and you are tempted to walk away from your faith in Christ.

Think! Where will you go? What will you do? Who else offers salvation and forgiveness of sins forever? Who else offers the strength you need?

For yet in a very little while, He who is coming will come, and will not delay. But My righteous one shall live by faith; and if he shrinks back, My soul has no pleasure in him. (Hebrews 10:37–38)

Shrinking back is the last thing you should do when you feel overwhelmed by devastating circumstances. That's the very time you need Jesus the most! Jesus understands the fire of affliction.

In fact, He is with you in the fire.

THE FOURTH MAN

In the Old Testament book of Daniel, we have a dramatic account of three young men who refused to compromise their faith in God, even in the face of terrible pressure and the threat of death.

Daniel chapter 3 tells the story of Nebuchadnezzar, the powerful king of Babylon, who crafted a great statue of gold and commanded everyone in his kingdom to bow down to the image at the sound of a certain musical prompt.

And by the way, this wasn't a suggestion or a request. It was a firm command, with serious consequences for noncompliance: "whoever does not fall down and worship shall be cast into the midst of a furnace of blazing fire" (v. 11).

You and I need to pay particular attention to this story of faith under persecution, for this is the kind of hurt I believe Christians in America may very well have to face one day. (Yes, I do believe followers of Jesus Christ in our own United States will face serious persecution in the not-too-distant future. We can see the beginnings of it already.)

The three Hebrew young men, perhaps no older than teenagers, had been given the Babylonian names of Shadrach, Meshach, and Abed-nego. As the account in Daniel reveals, they faced incredible pressure to conform, and it would have been so easy to simply go with the flow. Who would blame them, given the high stakes?

But when it came to loyalty to the true and living God, they simply would not compromise. No matter what.

Then Nebuchadnezzar in rage and anger

gave orders to bring Shadrach, Meshach and Abed-nego; then these men were brought before the king. Nebuchadnezzar responded and said to them, "Is it true, Shadrach, Meshach and Abed-nego, that you do not serve my gods or worship the golden image that I have set up? Now if you are ready, at the moment you hear the sound of the horn, flute, lyre, trigon, psaltery and bagpipe and all kinds of music, to fall down and worship the image that I have made, very well. But if you do not worship, you will immediately be cast into the midst of a furnace of blazing fire; and what god is there who can deliver you out of my hands?" (vv. 13–15)

It's an interesting question, isn't it? "What god is there who can deliver you out of my hands?"

Nebuchadnezzar seemed to think there was no god who could contend with him! And sometimes we ourselves buy this lie. We imagine that God is impotent and can't deliver us or He would never allow such hurt!

Do not forget what you have learned. God rules supreme. Satan cannot do anything without God's permission.

187

Consider the work of God,
  For who is able to straighten what He
  has bent?
In the day of prosperity be happy,
  But in the day of adversity consider —
  God has made the one as well as the
  other. (Ecclesiastes 7:13–14)

Do you feel the heat of the blazing furnace in your own life right now? Look at its glow; see its smoke. Don't turn away; it won't go away. Suffering goes hand in hand with following Jesus. Hurt is in your job description. "For to you it has been granted for Christ's sake, not only to believe in Him, but also to suffer for His sake" (Philippians 1:29).

I have a son who would love me if I would toe his line, if I would only change to fit what he thinks I ought to be and do. I could stay out of his furnace if I would bow — but if I did, it would mean I love my son more than I love my Lord!

And what about you, beloved? I know you have been willing to go into the furnace for the sake of your God. You refused to be unfaithful to your Lord and God — and I am proud of you.

Now let's see how these three young men responded to the king's threat.

Shadrach, Meshach and Abed-nego replied to the king, "O Nebuchadnezzar, we do not need to give you an answer concerning this matter. If it be so, our God whom we serve is able to deliver us from the furnace of blazing fire; and He will deliver us out of your hand, O king. But even if He does not, let it be known to you, O king, that we are not going to serve your gods or worship the golden image that you have set up." (Daniel 3:16–18)

Let it be known! And their faithfulness *was* known! Seen by all who stood there. Their fearless stand for God was witnessed by people who might have thought them absolute fools for defying the will of the king — or who were awed by so great a faith in their God.

Then Nebuchadnezzar was filled with wrath, and his facial expression was altered toward Shadrach, Meshach and Abed-nego. He answered by giving orders to heat the furnace seven times more than it was usually heated. He commanded certain valiant warriors who were in his army to tie up Shadrach, Meshach and Abed-nego in order to cast them into the furnace of blazing fire. Then these men were tied up in their trousers, their coats, their caps and their other clothes, and were cast into the midst of the furnace of blazing fire. For this reason, because the king's command was urgent and the furnace had been made extremely hot, the flame of the fire slew those men who carried up Shadrach, Meshach and Abed-nego. But these three men, Shadrach, Meshach and Abed-nego, fell into the midst of the furnace of blazing fire still tied up.

Then Nebuchadnezzar the king was astounded and stood up in haste; he said to his high officials, "Was it not three men we cast bound into the midst of the fire?" They replied to the king, "Certainly, O king." He said, "Look! I see four men loosed and walking about in the midst of the fire without harm, and the appearance of the fourth is like a son of the gods!" (vv. 19–25)

Remember the verses I urged you to memorize? *"I will never desert you, nor will I ever forsake you"* so that you may confidently say, *"The LORD is my helper"* (Hebrews 13:5–6). A helper? Oh yes! In fact, He was the fourth man in the fire!

The "never" and the "nor" are really five negatives in the original language: I will *never, never, never* leave you *nor never* forsake you! Have you got it? The reason we can say with the psalmist "I fear no evil" is that God walks with us through the valley of the shadow of death.[2]

Now watch what happened next:

Then Nebuchadnezzar came near to the door of the furnace of blazing fire; he responded and said, "Shadrach, Meshach and Abed-nego, come out, you servants of the Most High God, and come here!" Then Shadrach, Meshach and Abed-nego came out of the midst of the fire. The satraps, the prefects, the governors and the king's high officials gathered around and saw in regard to these men that the fire had no effect on the bodies of these men nor was the hair of their head singed, nor were their trousers damaged, nor had the smell of fire even come upon them.

Nebuchadnezzar responded and said, "Blessed be the God of Shadrach, Meshach and Abed-nego, who has sent His angel and delivered His servants who put their trust in Him, violating the king's command, and yielded up their bodies so as not to serve or worship any god except their own God." (Daniel 13:26–28)

Those valiant men came out without even smelling like smoke! And we can do the same. Rather than letting the odor of death or despair cling to us, we are to be a fragrance of Christ to all who come near us or hear about our faith.

But thanks be to God, who always leads us in triumph in Christ, and manifests through us the sweet aroma of the knowledge of Him in every place. For we are a fragrance of Christ to God among those who are being saved and among those who are perishing. (2 Corinthians 2:14–15)

We don't smell like the fire; we have the fragrance of the One who is with us in the fire.

JESUS UNDERSTANDS WHAT YOU'RE SUFFERING

Do you know one of the reasons for Jesus becoming a man?

He had to be made like His brethren in all things, so that He might become a merciful and faithful high priest in things pertaining to God, to make propitiation for the sins of the people. For since He Himself was tempted in that which He has suffered, He is able to come to the aid of those who are tempted. (Hebrews 2:17–18)

Remember, the Greek word *peirasmos,* translated in this passage as "tempted," could also be rendered as *tried* or *tested.* And so it is in our lives: suffering tries us, tests us, and tempts us, but because we are never alone and because Jesus has "been there," He understands. He is able to come to our aid and walk with us in the furnace of affliction.

Jesus knows what it is to groan, to cry, to shed tears.

In the days of His flesh, He offered up both prayers and supplications with loud crying and tears to the One able to save Him from death, and He was heard because of His piety. Although He was a Son, He learned obedience from the things which He suffered. (Hebrews 5:7–8)

Just about ten days ago, my husband, Jack, and I had lunch with a dear couple who at our request shared their incredible story of suffering. The husband had once headed up a church ministry that had been so blessed by God that it attracted national attention. But then jealousy raised its ugly head, and it all began to unravel. It reminded me of Saul's jealousy of David and his attempts to get rid of the younger man.

The husband had made a mistake in thinking his team could share leadership responsibilities, without any clear definition of roles and final authority. This lack of well-defined leadership structure provided an opportunity for individuals to act on their jealousy, and a coup was carried out during the couple's direly needed sabbatical.

Everything changed overnight.

Our friend was summarily removed as pastor of the church. Not only that, but he was made to jump through all sorts of hoops, a complicated process that ate up all of the couple's savings and left them virtually penniless.

Night after night this man and his prayer-warrior wife held each other and wept, until finally they ran out of tears. Under the crushing weight of this pain, they began to understand, perhaps for the first time, the deep pain of others. As a result, they felt a compassion for suffering and disadvantaged people beyond what they had ever experienced before.

Previously, when their busy lives gave them brief opportunities for fellowship with others, they'd spent their time with the leaders, those who supported the church financially rather than the rejects of society who had found life in Jesus through the church.

Now they'd been betrayed by those same leaders. The individuals who rallied around the hurting couple were the people who had lived through pain themselves, those who'd known the depths of depression and battled serious addictions. People who, after they were saved, chose to serve behind the scenes at the church. People who didn't care that their names were never mentioned in the bulletin, their contributions never recognized. They were just happy to be redeemed, set free, to love and serve Jesus wherever and however. These were the people who came around this couple — and who stood with them in the fire.

Eventually there were apologies from leaders in the church, along with confessions of wrongdoing and ungodly behavior. Yes, there were tears of repentance, but the fallout was great. The church has been struggling back from the brink, but God seems to have withdrawn His hand of favor.

The good news is that this couple and their children are stronger for what they went through. Though the pain has been great, their relationships are now deeper, their friendships are richer, and they are wiser. They now have a better grasp of God's principles of leadership, and they are determined to help others understand the thrill of the gospel. They've realized they had lessons to learn, and they are learning them!

They understand the prayers of Jesus, the loud crying and supplications, the tears . . . because they let Jesus walk with them in their suffering.

And what of you, beloved? Are you holding tightly to the hand of the One who walks with you in the fire? He is the God-man, the faithful Son over God's house. Hold fast your confidence.[3]

Remember that God wants you to cling to Him "as the waistband clings to the waist of a man," so that you might be a man, a woman of renown and glory in the eyes of your God (Jeremiah 13:11).

But now, thus says the LORD, your
   Creator, O Jacob,
  And He who formed you, O Israel,
   "Do not fear, for I have redeemed you;

I have called you by name; you are
Mine!
When you pass through the waters, I will
be with you;
And through the rivers, they will not
overflow you.
When you walk through the fire, you
will not be scorched,
Nor will the flame burn you." (Isaiah
43:1–2)

CHAPTER THIRTEEN:
THE LINGERING
HURT OF SUICIDE

"Murder-suicide."

How could two simple words contain so much gut-wrenching impact — such raw emotion and mind-bending incredulity?

"Murder-suicide."

The Georgia Bureau of Investigation employed those two words in their conclusion about the deaths of my dear friends, Nancy and Bruce Schaefer. Never, and I mean *never,* would anyone have imagined that these two lives might end in such a way. Bruce *killing his wife* of fifty-two years — and *then himself?* How could such a thing happen — ever?

Nancy was a woman whom I had known, loved, admired, and called a special friend for over thirty years. She was the founder of the ministry Family Concerns, had run for lieutenant governor of Georgia, and had served with distinction as a Georgia state senator. She had raised four sons and a daughter, was the grandmother of thirteen, and a woman who lived out the biblical precepts of a godly wife and mother in such an exemplary way. A woman of such courage and grace!

And she'd been shot dead in her sleep? *By her husband?*

If you'd asked me to give a one-word description of Bruce and Nancy's life, I would have used the word "beautiful," with no hesitation. Beautiful home in a gated community. Beautiful framed pictures of the family, gracing their tables. People who, by all outward appearances, lived a comfortable and beautiful life.

Murder-suicide didn't fit the picture of "beautiful."

Why did this happen? How could it happen? How could a life so faithfully lived for the Lord end this way?

Of course, those are the sorts of questions that always race through the mind when you hear an account of suicide. But for us, in this chapter, there are other important questions: What do you do when a tragedy like this touches your life and the life of your family? How do those left behind live with such a horrific circumstance?

I just used the word *tragedy.* And suicide is certainly that.

But it's also more than that.

Many deaths are tragedies, but this is a double tragedy. The passing of a loved one usually involves sorrow, but this is a double sorrow. You not only have to deal with an untimely death, you also have to deal with the wrenching, horrendous circumstances and implications of that death.

Think of all that the family of Bruce and Nancy had to process. Not only did they have to deal with the death of a father and grandfather by suicide, they also had to somehow work through the fact that he had decided to take their valiant, godly mother and grandmother away from them at the same time!

This was a man who had professed Jesus Christ as Savior — who for the last two years of his life had seemingly loved listening to his pastor teach the Word of God. It made no earthly sense at all.

Why would he . . . ?

How could he . . . ?

What was he thinking when he . . . ?

As I stood at the pulpit to speak at the funeral and looked down at that precious family and they at me, with two closed caskets covered with American flags between us, I knew we needed to address the situation exactly as it was.

Murder-suicide was the "elephant in the room," too big to ignore or to paper over with soothing platitudes. And besides, elephants have no place in the sanctuary of God!

The church auditorium and overflow room were filled with legislators, press, people from all walks of public service, and of course friends and family members who were still numb with bewilderment and sorrow over what had happened.

When the *Atlanta Journal-Constitution* ran a story about the service, they quoted me as saying, "They didn't go the way we expected them to go, but they went, and they went to God Almighty. Don't think of the way they died, think of the way they lived." The wording wasn't quite accurate, but they did capture the truth that our focus must not be on death but on life.

At the close of the service, and in the days that followed, people expressed appreciation that I had addressed the situation as it was. In other words, that I had spoken to the "elephant in the room."

That's what this chapter will attempt to do as well.

I don't believe there can be any real healing until we bring God into the tragedy and find out how He would have us live when the hurt just couldn't go any deeper.

THOUGHTS IN THE DARK

Have you ever thought about taking your own life?

If you have, why did such a thought ever cross your mind? Can you remember why you wanted to? Why you didn't? How God met you at that wilderness crossroads and helped you make the right turns and take the right paths?

There have been three times in my own life when I contemplated suicide.

The first time was before I became an honest-to-goodness Christian with a changed life to prove it. My dreams of a happy marriage and family had turned out to be just that: dreams, not reality. Tom, the man for whom I had saved my virginity, was bipolar. I hadn't understood that and didn't have a clue what to do about it. I didn't know how to handle his constant criticism, his endless unhappiness, or his frightening descents into depression and despair.

The second contemplation of suicide came after I was saved. No matter what anyone may tell you, divorce and immorality invariably bring powerful and corrosive consequences. There are aftereffects that have the potential to cause heartache for your children for years to come. One of my grown sons had refused to forgive me because he didn't have the "perfect" life he longed for. (I longed for it too!) The thought came, *What better way to let your son know how deeply he is hurting you than by killing yourself in his home? Hang yourself in the bathroom.*

But then what would it do to my sons? Especially to the two who lost their father on a rope on a closet door? My love for them overtook my twisted thinking.

The third time occurred while I was visiting my widowed mother. Someone from the office called to tell me that our women's conference was taking place that very weekend, not the next as I had thought, and I was the keynote speaker.

Just that quickly all the pressures and responsibilities in my life at that moment seemed to break over my head like a tidal wave, and I felt utterly overwhelmed. Flattened. Drowning.

I remember walking from the kitchen to the bedroom where I was staying, when the thought clearly entered my mind: *Why don't you just kill yourself? It will be all over then. You'll just die and go to heaven. What could be better?*

Within moments, I recognized the voice.

It had the characteristic "hiss" of the serpent of old, the devil, Satan. It was the voice of the one Jesus identified not only as a liar, but as the very "father of lies" and a "murderer from the beginning" (John 8:44).

Of course the archenemy of God would love to see a Christian with an established ministry commit suicide. Think of the press, the buzz, the speculations, the questions, the doubts, and the accusations. The enemy could have a heyday if someone who had so publically proclaimed the Lord — His Word, His grace, His sufficiency, His power, His sovereignty — made the decision to destroy herself. And there would be those who would ask themselves, *Is God sufficient or not for any and every situation of life?*

Those who commit suicide often see it as the way out of pain, the solution to a problem rather than the ending of life. It's also a way of sending a message, of letting people know the depths we've plumbed — and their role in it all. It is a totally self-absorbed act and an out-and-out denial of the sufficiency of God.

In essence, when a person commits suicide, they're usurping God, just like the devil of old. According to the Bible, the power of life and death belong to only one: God. He wounds, He heals. He kills, He makes alive, and He numbers our days.[1] He is the One who does these things, and He alone has the right to do so because He is God.

Honestly, I don't think there is anything harder to deal with than having a loved one commit suicide.

Why? Why? Why? It's all you can think, all you can ask, all you can repeat over and over again. *Why didn't you talk to me? Why didn't you tell me how bad it was? If you had only told me, we could have figured something out . . . resolved it . . . talked it through . . . found some help . . .*

Left to deal with the aftermath, you feel utterly impotent! You just know something could have been done. But you weren't given a chance. And now you're left with no options. No second chances. Your loved one is gone, leaving you to bear their pain as well as your own. This is a hurt that runs deeper than you ever thought possible.

Sooner or later you want answers, help, someone to talk to — preferably someone who has been there and appears to have survived.

I am often contacted by people who heard that my first husband killed himself. They're seeking information for themselves or a friend, and they can't find much on the subject. And more often than not, they have questions about God. How does God fit with suicide? We'll talk about that in a minute, but first let me tell you about the suicide of my husband and what God taught me through it.

TOM'S SUICIDE

I married Tom at age twenty, and we divorced six years later, by which time we had two sons. At age twenty-nine, I became a child of God. It was soon after this that Tom committed suicide.

At the time, I was so young in the Lord that I can't even remember praying and asking God to show me what to tell my sons. But I do remember calling my parents, telling them what had happened, and asking them if I could leave the boys with them while I went to Cleveland, Ohio, for the funeral. My two sons were young — too young, my parents thought, to handle the concept of the father they loved taking his own life. So we told them he was sick and died. It wasn't until they were older that I finally told them. Little did I realize the emotional havoc it would play in the hearts and minds of these boys who so dearly loved their daddy.

As I mentioned earlier, Tom was manic

depressive, bipolar, and we didn't know it. I didn't understand much about the condition, even though I was working at Toledo State Mental Hospital when Tom and I were dating. All I knew was how hard it was to please him, that sometimes nothing could make him happy, and how he would so often simply come home, eat, and then go right to bed.

Tom had been an incredible athlete, voted most likely to succeed, intellectually at genius level, poised, good looking, a great dancer, and a good lover. He was faithful in our marriage, interested in God, and fully responsible to provide for his family.

I just couldn't understand why he was so overwhelmingly restless and bitterly unhappy. It made no sense to me as a young woman, and I simply wasn't prepared to deal with that reality. So I listened to the ungodly, unbiblical counsel of two clergymen and left him.

In those three years between our divorce and my salvation, Tom would call me and tell me he was thinking of suicide. I did the only thing I had ever been taught to do in such a circumstance — try to bluff him out of it, or make him so mad he wouldn't do it.

So I would say, "Do a good job, so I get

your money." Or, "Why don't you fly your plane into the side of a mountain so I can get your insurance?"

How absolutely horrible — to tell someone his life is worth money! But as I said, I was lost and didn't fully comprehend the destructive power in my own words. The Bible says the tongue is a little member, but set on fire by hell!²

After I came to know the Lord, I told God I would go back to Tom, because I knew God hated divorce. In fact, I was all prepared to do so.

Then the phone call came. It was my father-in-law, saying, "Tom is dead, Kay. He hung himself."

I hung up the phone, fell down on my knees beside the bed, and grabbed the phone again. I called my pastor, but he didn't answer. How thankful I am that he wasn't home! Why? Because the next thing I did was cry out to God with all my heart. I can't remember what I said to my heavenly Father, but I do remember what He said to me, the thoughts He put in my mind.

He gave me three things from His Word, the Bible.

First, *"in everything give thanks,"* to which I replied, "I don't understand why, but thank You."³

The second thing that came to my mind was *"I won't give you anything you cannot bear."* I had just memorized 1 Corinthians 10:13 in the King James Version, printed on a card and distributed by the Navigators:

There hath no temptation *[trial or testing]* taken you but such as is common to man: but God is faithful, who will not suffer you to be tempted above that ye are able; but will with the temptation also make a way to escape, that ye may be able to bear it.

God's assurance from that promise welled up in my heart. I could make it. Our little family would survive.

The third thing was, *"I will use this for your good."* Later, I would find this hope woven through the promise of God in Romans 8:28–30.[4] I didn't know those verses then, but I knew that God, through His indwelling Spirit, had spoken peace and strength into my mind. I felt Him nudging me to believe in Him and cling to Him — even in that terrible moment. And from that point on, that's what I did. This would be my healing, my strength, my sanity — my victory!

When I went to Tom's apartment, an

apartment I had never seen, I walked over and looked at the hall closet door where he had hung himself. After all these years I can still see it.

On his bedside table, I picked up something he had evidently torn from the Sunday supplement of the newspaper. It was a poem about God.

At the funeral, I walked down the aisle of the church and sat in the first pew. Looking at the coffin through the black veil of my hat, my mind went back to another veil and our wedding pictures. The coffin was where we stood and made our vows — "until death us do part."

Have I missed Tom? Honestly — yes. Have I thought about him? Occasionally. Do I wonder how different my life would have been had I gone back? I've started to go there in my thoughts, but I know better. Do I wish I had asked God how to tell my sons about their father's passing, instead of relying on the opinions of others? Very much. Are there tears in my eyes as I type this? Yes. But there's also a deep abiding peace in my heart, because I know this is the will of God in Christ Jesus. God is sovereign, not only over life but over death. I bow my knees.

WHAT YOU NEED TO KNOW

So how do you deal with the questions that suicide inevitably brings?

First, you need to understand the destination of the one who took his life. Many have been taught that suicide sends a person to hell. This conclusion, however, simply doesn't line up with the Word of God.

The fact that an individual takes his life does not consign the person to hell. A person's eternal destination is determined by how he has responded to the offer of salvation in Jesus Christ during his lifetime, not by whether or not he took his own life. When an individual truly repents at any point in his life, believing that Jesus is the Christ, the Son of God who paid for our sins through His death and was raised on the third day, that person is saved and has the promise of eternal life. This is what the Word of God says. Of course, there will also be evidence of a changed life, as the New Testament makes clear in passages such as 1 Corinthians 6:9–11, Ephesians 5:1–5, Galatians 5:19–24, and the book of 1 John.

At death, all true children of God are absent from the body and immediately present with the Lord.[5] Some who commit suicide know this and take their own lives with this confidence. The thing they forget is that they must stand before the Lord and give an account for what they have done and how they have usurped God. By taking their own life, they have belied the sufficiency of His grace and the truth of His promises. Suicide is not a valiant way for a child of God to die; in fact, it is shameful.

So how do we know that a Christian who commits suicide is with God? Because of what Jesus — the only Savior — taught. Listen to His words as He addressed some Jews near the portico of Solomon on the temple mount. It was winter, the time of the Feast of Dedication. If you have your pencil handy, you might want to underline every reference to Jesus, and circle every reference to *His* sheep. It will help you observe His words more closely and accurately. By the way, take off your personal theological glasses and simply take Jesus at His word. His every word is truth, and He never contradicts Himself!

The Jews then gathered around Him, and were saying to Him, "How long will You keep us in suspense? If You are the Christ, tell us plainly."

Jesus answered them, "I told you, and you do not believe; the works that I do in My Father's name, these testify of

Me. But you do not believe because you are not of My sheep. My sheep hear My voice, and I know them, and they follow Me; and I give eternal life to them, and they will never perish; and no one will snatch them out of My hand. My Father, who has given them to Me, is greater than all; and no one is able to snatch them out of the Father's hand. I and the Father are one." (John 10:24–30)

Now what do you learn about Jesus' sheep in these verses? Jesus' sheep believe and listen to His voice because they are *His* sheep. The Father gave them to Jesus. Jesus knows His own and gives them eternal life. They will *never* perish and no one — absolutely no one, including themselves — can pluck them out of Jesus' hand. Jesus who is one with the Father, together with His Father, keeps His sheep!

Do you remember the e-mail I shared early in the book from the widow whose son had committed suicide and whose young daughter was so ill? She wrote, "Why do these things happen? I had it all. We were the perfect Christian family, happy, serving God, loving each other. Now we are left with rubble. Does God care?"

I want to put my arms around this woman

and say, "Yes, yes, precious one, He cares. Why it happened, I have no idea. But what I do know is that God is there and that He cares. He gave the life of His Son for the life of your son. He raised Jesus from the dead, to die no more, and it will be the same for your boy.

"Because your dear son is a child of God, God was there for him. And although he took his own life, God let it happen. You will see him again, because Jesus is the resurrection and the life and 'He who believes in Me will live even if he dies' (John 11:25).

"Know, precious one, God will not leave you, nor forsake you. Cling to Him and to His promises, and let Him comfort you with the comfort only He can give. Heaven awaits, and God Himself will wipe away your tears, because He cares. At least you have the assurance of your son's faith and the knowledge that you *will* see him again. You may not understand very many things right now, but *that* you can know."

To that dear woman and to you, I offer this encouragement, straight from the mouth of Jesus:

"I am the bread of life; he who comes to Me will not hunger, and he who believes in Me will never thirst. But I said to you that you have seen Me, and yet do not believe. All that the Father gives Me will come to Me, and the one who comes to Me I will certainly not cast out. For I have come down from heaven, not to do My own will, but the will of Him who sent Me. This is the will of Him who sent Me, that of all that He has given Me I lose nothing, but raise it up on the last day. For this is the will of My Father, that everyone who beholds the Son and believes in Him will have eternal life, and I Myself will raise him up on the last day. . . .

"No one can come to Me unless the Father who sent Me draws him; and I will raise him up on the last day." (John 6:35–40, 44)

What is the bottom line for everyone who dies — by whatever means? Those given to the Son by the Father will never, ever be lost but will be raised up on the last day! Their bodies will be resurrected and united with their souls, just as the apostle Paul declares in 1 Thessalonians 4:13–18.

Jesus is not only the Lamb of God who takes away the sins of the world; He is the good shepherd of sheep given by the Father from every nation. You will see this again as you circle each reference to His sheep in the following verses:

"I am the good shepherd, and I know My own and My own know Me, even as the Father knows Me and I know the Father; and I lay down My life for the sheep. I have other sheep, which are not of this fold; I must bring them also, and they will hear My voice; and they will become one flock with one shepherd. For this reason the Father loves Me, because I lay down My life so that I may take it again. No one has taken it away from Me, but I lay it down on My own initiative. I have authority to lay it down, and I have authority to take it up again. This commandment I received from My Father." (John 10:14–18)

This passage includes one of the most wonderful verses you will ever read. Why? Because with the words "I have other sheep, which are not of this fold," Jesus showed that His sheep included more than the small circle of His disciples and the Jews who would put their trust in Him. With this verse, Jesus also wrapped His saving arm around you and me, Gentiles, the sheep of another fold.

Jesus was so confident of these truths that He prayed them back to the Father on His way to the Garden of Gethsemane, shortly before His arrest.

Jesus spoke these things; and lifting up His eyes to heaven, He said, "Father, the hour has come; glorify Your Son, that the Son may glorify You, even as You gave Him authority over all flesh, that to all whom You have given Him, He may give eternal life. This is eternal life, that they may know You, the only true God, and Jesus Christ whom You have sent. I glorified You on the earth, having accomplished the work which You have given Me to do. Now, Father, glorify Me together with Yourself, with the glory which I had with You before the world was." (John 17:1–5)

Whatever way a person dies, God will not lose those He drew to Himself through His Son, Jesus Christ. They will live again. Jesus accomplished His purpose.

And if a person dies, by whatever means, without receiving Jesus Christ? Where is that person? According to Jesus in Luke 16:19–31, the unbeliever is in Hades, eternally separated from God, and will spend eternity in the lake of fire where the worm dies not and the fire is not quenched.[6]

This is a hard truth, but it is truth. Jesus came to die for all mankind, but those in Hades are there because they refused to believe this and rejected Jesus Christ as their Lord and Savior. No human being can come to the Father except through Jesus Christ.

Just remember, beloved, there is no other savior. You are not the savior. You cannot save anyone, but you are responsible to share the gospel, the good news of salvation through the Son of God.

If an individual dies without believing, you can know that even if they had lived for a thousand years, they never would have become a true child of God. This is what Jesus was teaching: He never loses one of His sheep.

So how do those of us left behind live with the tragedy of suicide? Let me share seven precepts for you to consider. You might think of them as seven handholds of faith in the midst of the storm.

SEVEN HANDHOLDS OF FAITH
1. For reasons we may not understand, God allowed this.

Because God is God, because He is sovereign, because He holds the keys to hell and death, we have to understand that ultimately, God allowed the death. Sometimes God thwarts suicide attempts, but in this case, He didn't. He chose not to intervene. Furthermore, if there is no suicide note, no clear evidence, it serves no purpose to wear your mind out trying to guess or speculate on all the "whys" of any given suicide.

Although God has all knowledge, there are some things He simply doesn't let us know . . . yet. So don't try to "finish the picture" or fill in details that may never be in your possession in this life. Why? Because the enemy of your soul will exploit your anxious, tortured thoughts in an attempt to turn you away from the peace and rest that only God can give you.

Face the reality of what happened, without trying to cover it with drugs, alcohol, anger, rebellion, bitter remorse, isolation, or endless speculation. Instead, turn to the living God and let Him comfort you through His Word and through wise and godly friends. God will work this together for your good, if you are His. And if not, then become a true child of God, and watch Him begin to do that very thing.

2. Seek the companionship of the Lord.

There is no comforter, no companion in all the world like Jesus. He will never leave you. He will never forsake you. He is your helper (see Hebrews 13:5–6).

I've heard people say after a suicide, "If my loved one is in hell, then I want to go there too to be with him, to be with her."

No, you don't.

You would change your mind after a thousandth of a second. And there is no fellowship in hell. It is a place of ultimate, eternal separation and isolation — not just from God, but from one another.

Seek the company of heaven. Desire the companionship of the Father, Son, and Holy Spirit. Join the psalmist in declaring, "Whom have I in heaven but You? And besides You, I desire nothing on earth. . . . God is the strength of my heart and my portion forever. . . . As for me, the nearness of God is my good. I have made the Lord GOD my refuge" (Psalm 73:25–28).

3. Face the facts.

Face the facts of what actually happened. Put God at your side and deal with it. Yes,

220

talk to your friends and let them comfort you, but carefully measure everything they say with the Word of God. Separate the precious from the worthless.

4. Go ahead and grieve.

Weep, wail, mourn. Express your frustration, your anger, your disappointment, your sorrow, and your pain. There is cause for that. But then, after a brief season, put it away, and go forward with life and God. As the old King James Bible put it, "Weeping may endure for a night, but joy cometh in the morning" (Psalm 30:5). Remember the three things the Spirit of God shared with me when my husband committed suicide, which I spoke of earlier in this chapter. Review those words, and then cling to them.

5. Don't continually revisit the details.

You can't bring your loved one back, and you can't change what has already happened. So why go there in your mind? The past is past. Absolutely nothing can change or reverse it. God has it covered, and you need to leave it with Him.

To revisit traumatic events over and over will not profit you a thing and will only bring undue, unnecessary stress to your mind and body.

Walk literally in the light of the sun, as darkness will only increase depression, and walk literally in the light of His truth, which will bring healing.[7] Open the curtains in your house and let the light in. Open the curtains of your heart and let the healing and life of His Word flow in.

Let me take you to one passage that is sufficient, although you will find many others as you nurture your soul on the bread of His Word. It is found in Philippians, sometimes called "the epistle of joy." Read it aloud. Post it on the mirror, the refrigerator, beside your bed, or where you have your quiet time with the Lord. Memorize it, and let its healing seep into the crevices of your soul.

Finally, brethren, whatever is true, whatever is honorable, whatever is right, whatever is pure, whatever is lovely, whatever is of good repute, if there is any excellence and if anything worthy of praise, dwell on these things. The things you have learned and received and heard and seen in me, practice these things, and the God of peace will be with you. (4:8–9)

Bring every thought against the plumb

line of the eight qualifications of Philippians 4:8, and if the thought doesn't measure up to these, then simply don't go there. This is the way I have dealt with every sorrowful event and with remembrances that sometimes seek to invade my mind. What torment I avoid, and what peace I enjoy! It is not denial; it is *obedience,* and God will bless it. Remember that.

6. Time and practicing His truth will bring healing.

Imitate the apostle Paul and do as he did in Philippians 3:13–14: ". . . Forgetting what lies behind and reaching forward to what lies ahead, I press on toward the goal for the prize of the upward call of God in Christ Jesus."

Your life has purpose, beloved. It is not finished, and that is why you are still alive. So ask God to teach you to number your days that you might apply your heart to wisdom and get on with His purpose for your life.

7. Finally, comfort others with the comfort God has given you.

That was the conclusion Paul came to, as he related a deeply distressing season in which he also had despaired of life. In the midst of it all, he found the comfort of God, and the God of all comfort. And he realized that good could come of His sharing that comfort with others.

I would so love to take you into my arms and pray with you.

You will be all right, and more than all right. The healing that is beginning in your heart this very moment will grow and grow until it finally overflows and spills over into the lives of others.

CHAPTER FOURTEEN:
PULLING THE PLUG ON PAIN

"Kay, we're going to pull the plug on Mike."

Mike was Gene and Billie's wayward son, a precious young man with wonderful, loving parents, who nevertheless fell into the world of drugs and addiction as a teenager and could not climb back out again.

For a while — a short, beautiful season — it seemed as if things had changed. Mike, now in his forties, had been drug-free for months, and it looked as though the prayers stored before the Father's throne were finally being answered. They had their son back.

But then his body got sick and just couldn't seem to recover. All the tubes running into Mike's body couldn't jump-start him back to life so that he could make it on his own. After waiting weeks for his body to respond, it was finally time to let him go.

Jack and I stood with our friends by Mike's hospital bed, and I held Billie's hand in mine. Our hearts ached for them. Our friends have an extraordinary love for God, and I've often wondered if it's because they have experienced such deep hurt in their lives.

Mike had left a wake of pain as he careened recklessly through life, and Gene and Billie rode the waves, trusting God through their tears. In the process, they became examples to Jack and me and to many, many others as well.

Yet for all their strength in Christ, and all their heart assurance about God and His sovereignty, it wasn't easy to pull the plug.

Is it ever?

Pulling the plug implies letting go, moving on, and finally acknowledging that something once treasured — a life, a relationship, a dream for the future — has come to an end. It's over. It's relinquished — hopefully to God!

But how do you do it — pull the plug on hurt and sorrow?

- How do you deal with chronic physical pain and still find some way to be content?
- How do you handle the hurt of your loved one with Alzheimer's who no longer knows you and whom you can-

not safely keep at home?

- How do you process the death of a child, a mate, or a parent — someone who shared your life and home?
- How do you live with the knowledge that a baby never saw the light of day because you had an abortion? How can you keep from remembering that the child would be so many years old this year, if you hadn't done what you did?
- How do you release the pain of being married to someone who has promised over and over that the infidelity would stop but it hasn't? You are worn, weary, and determined to be faithful to your vows before God, knowing very well that He hates divorce. But how long should it go on?

When, if ever, do you release that hurt, let it go, and walk away? And once you make such a decision, how do you really live that way and move forward in life?

Let's look at the Scriptures and see if we can glean any precepts for life on this.

A LESSON IN LETTING GO

Genesis 22 is such an incredible chapter that has taught me so much about living and about God. But before we go there, let me get you up to speed on what has happened with Abraham, the main character in the story, up to this point.

God had promised a son to Abraham and his wife, Sarah. Having a son was a must if Abraham was to become the father of a new nation as God had promised. Remember, as we've already noted, all the nations of the earth were to be blessed through God's promise to Abraham.[1] The promise came when Abraham was seventy-five and Sarah, ten years his junior.

And then they waited and waited and waited. After twenty-five years of waiting, there was still no baby.

When Paul wrote to the church in Rome, laying out the constitution of our faith, he used Abraham as the supreme example of righteousness through faith. In doing so, he touted Abraham's faith and hope against hope:

In hope against hope he believed, so that he might become a father of many nations according to that which had been spoken, "So shall your descendants be." Without becoming weak in faith he contemplated his own body, now as good as dead since he was about a hundred years old, and the deadness of

228

Sarah's womb; yet, with respect to the promise of God, he did not waver in unbelief but grew strong in faith, giving glory to God, and being fully assured that what God had promised, He was able also to perform. Therefore it was also credited to Him as righteousness. (Romans 4:18–22)

When he finally arrived, Isaac was a miracle baby, because both Abraham and Sarah were well past the years when they might have hoped for a pregnancy. They had waited twenty-five years for this baby boy.

Why do I share this with you now? Because you need to understand how very special Isaac was to this elderly couple. He was their only son and their only connection to the future. I also want you to see that Abraham was a man of faith, a man who knew his God. Abraham's God was a *big* God — God Almighty!

When we reach Genesis 22, Isaac, the promised son, has grown up into a sturdy young man, and he is everything Abraham and Sarah dreamed of and could have wished for.

And at that moment God chose to make a shocking and heartrending request.

Let's read the first portion of Genesis 22

and see what God asked of Abraham and why I am using him as an illustration for "pulling the plug," or letting go.

If you have your pen or pencil in hand, why don't you put a heart over the word *love*. It is the first time the word is used in the Bible. You might also want to draw a cloud around *worship,* as it is the first time that word is used in Scripture. And one more: the word *obey* also appears for the first time. Circle that word.

> Now it came about after these things, that God tested Abraham, and said to him, "Abraham!" And he said, "Here I am." He said, "Take now your son, your only son, whom you love, Isaac, and go to the land of Moriah, and offer him there as a burnt offering on one of the mountains of which I will tell you." So Abraham rose early in the morning and saddled his donkey, and took two of his young men with him and Isaac his son; and he split wood for the burnt offering, and arose and went to the place of which God had told him. (vv. 1–3)

There is a great deal here that the Bible does *not* say, and when God does not say, we are not supposed to add our own ideas about how Abraham felt. We're simply told, "Abraham rose up early and saddled his donkey." In other words, he obeyed.

On the third day Abraham raised his eyes and saw the place from a distance. Abraham said to his young men, "Stay here with the donkey, and I and the lad will go over there; and we will worship and return to you." Abraham took the wood of the burnt offering and laid it on Isaac his son, and he took in his hand the fire and the knife. So the two of them walked on together. (vv. 4–6)

Again, the Bible tells us little about that walk up Mount Moriah, except to relate a conversation between father and son:

Isaac spoke to Abraham his father and said, "My father!" And he said, "Here I am, my son." And he said, "Behold, the fire and the wood, but where is the lamb for the burnt offering?" Abraham said, "God will provide for Himself the lamb for the burnt offering, my son." So the two of them walked on together.
Then they came to the place of which God had told him; and Abraham built the altar there and arranged the wood,

and bound his son Isaac and laid him on the altar, on top of the wood. (vv. 7–9)

Are you cringing, wondering how a loving father could possibly do this to his son? Please stay with me, friend, and it will become clear.

Abraham stretched out his hand and took the knife to slay his son. But the angel of the LORD called to him from heaven and said, "Abraham, Abraham!" And he said, "Here I am." He said, "Do not stretch out your hand against the lad, and do nothing to him; for now I know that you fear God, since you have not withheld your son, your only son, from Me." . . .
So Abraham returned to his young men, and they arose and went together to Beersheba; and Abraham lived at Beersheba. (vv. 10–12, 19)

Did you see it? Why I used this as an illustration? In this real-life account, God asked Abraham to completely, unreservedly release his grip on the whole centerpiece of his life — Isaac, the link to a nation from Abraham's seed! *Take your son, your only son whom you love! Offer him as a sacrifice!*

Let him go!"

What I want you to see is that Abraham *obeyed* God as an act of *worship.* Thinking back to Job, he too worshiped after releasing his grip on everything he held dear.

Oh beloved, I cannot stress it enough: God is our all in all.[2] "For from Him and through Him and to Him are all things. To Him be the glory forever. Amen" (Romans 11:36).

We have to know God inside and out. We have to know Him in all His fullness and in everything He reveals about Himself in His Word. This is the only way we can respond in faith when He asks us to pull the plug on what we have longed for.

This knowledge enables us to obey out of love and *as an act of worship,* confident that God is working for our ultimate good even through our present pain. It is the obedience of faith.

Listen to what Hebrews 11 tells us about this time in Abraham's life:

By faith Abraham, when he was tested, offered up Isaac, and he who had received the promises was offering up his only begotten son; it was he to whom it was said, "In Isaac your descendants shall be called." He considered that God

233

is able to raise people even from the dead, from which he also received him back as a type. (vv. 17–19)

Abraham's willingness to sacrifice his son was a type, or foreshadowing, of another, future sacrifice.

Do you remember when God pulled the plug, so to speak, on the life of His Son — His only begotten Son whom He loved? It's interesting, isn't it, that the first time the word *love* is used in the Bible, it is in connection with a father — Abraham — offering his only begotten son whom he loved. Do you see the connection between the two events?

It's also interesting to consider how hard it must have been on our Father when Jesus asked Him three times to take the cup of death from Him. We witness Jesus' act of worship and obedience as He said, in the very next breath, "Yet not My will, but Yours be done" (Luke 22:42). How difficult it must have been for Jesus to let go and surrender His very body and life. And how hard it must have been for both Father and Son to endure that moment when Jesus cried from the cross, "Eli, Eli, . . . My God, My God, why have You forsaken Me?" (Matthew 27:46).

The death of the only begotten Son of God, however, was the only way for us to be saved — for Abraham's seed to become like the sand of the sea and the stars of heaven.

And what does this have to do with your decision to unclench your fingers and release your grip on your love, your hope, your dream, your future, and let it go?

What Abraham did, what Jesus did, and what God did, all brought about God's purpose. Yet in each case, God's purposes seemed to run counter to human understanding.

It was the grace of God — grace through faith — that gave Abraham back his son "resurrected."[3] It was the obedience of Jesus dying as the payment for our sins that enabled you and me to be saved by grace through faith, and for God to raise Jesus from the dead. And of course it was love and grace that caused God to give His only begotten Son so that we would not be lost forever, without hope and without God.

In every case, the choice to let go — the willingness to pull the plug on personal dreams and desires — made way for God's grace to do its healing work.

LETTING GO OF DISCONTENT

There came a time in the life of the apostle Paul when he pleaded with God for healing from a troubling physical affliction. Instead, God gave His servant the grace and power to pull the plug on that cry of his heart.

Read the passage below out loud, and listen to it with the ears of faith:

Because of the surpassing greatness of the revelations, for this reason, to keep me from exalting myself, there was given me a thorn in the flesh, a messenger of Satan to torment me — to keep me from exalting myself! Concerning this I implored the Lord three times that it might leave me. And He has said to me, "My grace is sufficient for you, for power is perfected in weakness." Most gladly, therefore, I will rather boast about my weaknesses, so that the power of Christ may dwell in me. Therefore I am well content with weaknesses, with insults, with distresses, with persecutions, with difficulties, for Christ's sake; for when I am weak, then I am strong. (2 Corinthians 12:7–10)

Did you notice, beloved, that the thorn was "a messenger of Satan"? And to whom did Paul go to get relief from this messenger of Satan? God!

What does that tell you about Paul's theology — his belief in God and understanding of God? Paul knew God was sovereign, even over Satan. He asked God three times to remove the troubling thorn, even as Jesus asked His father three times to take the cup from Him.

And what was God's answer? The Greek verb form Paul used in the phrase "And He has said" is in the perfect tense, indicating a completed action with a present and continuous result. Which means God said, "This is my final answer!" In essence, God's final answer to Paul was this: "The thorn is staying, but My grace is sufficient to help you live with the thorn intact." God's power (and that's what grace is) is seen, completed, experienced, and brought to fullness in our weaknesses.

Do you see?

You *can* live with a "thorn."

You can live with whatever you're going through right now that God won't stop or take away. The "thorn" will not destroy you. In fact, as you allow it to serve its intended purpose in your life, you may experience God's power in a way you have never experienced it before! You can handle that thing, that challenge, that heartache, that hurt "according to the power that works within us" (Ephesians 3:20), a power not your own.

This is a power that will actually make you want to boast about your "weaknesses," because it demonstrates the power of grace that you might not otherwise experience. It's the thorn, the hurt, that causes you to turn to divine power. It is power that you don't earn or merit but is made available to you because of the life of Jesus within you. For that reason, you can bear whatever comes your way, saying with Paul, "I can do all things through Him who strengthens me" (Philippians 4:13).

HEALING TRUTH #10

God's grace is brought to fullness in our lives as we release our hurt and draw on His power in our weakness.

So what does Paul do that we should also do? We are to pull the plug on the hurt and, letting go of what *we* want, move on to contentment. Let's read it again, and hear it in our innermost being, fixing it on our heart: "Therefore I am well content with weaknesses, with insults, with distresses, with persecutions, with difficulties, for Christ's sake; for when I am weak, then I am strong" (2 Corinthians 12:10).

How contrary this is to our natural tendency, but only by pulling the plug on our natural selves, on our fleshly desires, can we experience in full the supernatural grace and power of God.

LETTING GO OF WHAT MIGHT HAVE BEEN

It was the sufficiency of God's grace, His power that enabled Gene and Billie to disconnect their much-loved son, Mike, from life support. They had asked for Mike's life, but God had said no to them more than once. And if you ever want to see firsthand the power of grace perfected in weakness, then you want to take Gene and Billie out for coffee someday and hear their story from their own lips. As deep as their hurt has been, they live in the peace of absolute trust.

The death of a loved one — spouse, parent, dear friend — leaves such a gaping hole in our lives, no matter the circumstances. But when death comes to a young child, the family is often overwhelmed by thoughts of what might have been if only the young life

had been allowed to blossom into adult-
hood.

David and Nancy Guthrie's last two
children were born with serious congenital
defects. As a result, these parents would
only have 199 days to hold and love their
daughter, Hope. Two and a half years later,
they would be given only 183 days with
their son, Gabriel.[4]

Twice they endured this inexplicable loss.
And although it hurt so badly, God has used
the Guthries' story and testimony as their
books have been translated into eight languages and have ministered to thousands
around the world.

Because the Guthries chose to pull the
plug on their pain — to not continue nurtur-
ing it with *if onlys* — and were willing to
walk in the sufficiency and power of God's
grace, many suffering, grieving people have
found strong comfort in their pain.

PULLING THE PLUG ON GUILT

The Guthries' babies died though Dave and
Nancy did everything possible to keep them
alive. But what if your baby died by your
own choice, and you aborted the child
conceived safely in your womb? Or what if
you are the man whose baby was aborted
because you wanted it done? Can you ever

pull the plug on the pain and guilt? You know you took a life. I don't have to tell you about the shame, the depth of remorse, the late-night thoughts of how old the child would be now *if only* . . .

Do you feel guilt every time the word *abortion* is mentioned? Do you want to run from the room or stop up your ears? Do you find yourself wondering if the hurt will *ever* go away?

I only understand, dear one, because I have listened to so many women describe the pain carved into their hearts by a choice they so deeply regret.

Before I was a Christian, and when I was divorced from my first husband, Tom, we slept together when he came to see the boys. And then . . . my period was late. Was I pregnant? At the time, I was a nurse at Johns Hopkins and friends with some ob-gyn doctors, so we rigged a D and C — which in my case was for all intents and purposes an abortion, since there was no real justification for such a procedure.

It turned out that I wasn't pregnant. But I had been fully willing to kill the child I thought was in my womb. So what does that say? Only that, while I can't fully know your sorrow as I wasn't pregnant, I too stand guilty.

So what do you do? I believe you need to pull the plug on your hurt. Let it go and be healed.

"But," you say, "I took a life."

Yes, beloved, you did.

Hang on now, for I'm going to speak very frankly. I want to share with you how to pull the plug on this hurt that reaches into the depths of your heart and spreads its tumor-like tentacles through your mind.

You broke God's law. God says, "You shall not murder" (Deuteronomy 5:17), but you did. You knowingly, willfully chose to take the life within you, a life that God Himself had placed there. You sinned against God.

Have you confessed it? Called it murder? Asked God to forgive you? And has He? He promises He will, in 1 John 1:9. Or have you somehow believed a lie, that this is beyond the scope of Christ's blood and God's forgiveness?

Would God lie? *Can* God lie? If He promised to forgive you for all your sins and cleanse you from all unrighteousness, as we've discussed in this book, has He in fact done that?

Yes, He has. You can stake your life on it.

Remember, God sees your *heart*. The words of your confession don't have to be said a certain way. It's not some perfectly spoken word combination that unlocks His forgiveness; it is a heart that agrees with Him on what sin is.

Do you agree that abortion is a sin? Then if you confessed it as such, what has God done? He does what He says. God watches over His word to perform it.[5] He has forgiven you, absolutely and completely.

Now, is there any more you can do?

Please don't tell me you can't forgive yourself. Forgiving yourself is *not* in the Bible, and it's *not* an issue. Sometimes we confuse forgiving ourselves with forgetting what we did. While we may have to live with the memory of our sins, as far as God is concerned, they're *gone.* Psalm 103:12 tells us that "As far as the east is from the west, so far has He removed our transgressions from us."

Dear reader, let this hurt go. With God's help, release it.

Thank Him for forgiving you and for *completely* cleansing you of all unrighteousness. Thank Him that your baby is with Him, which is the best place anyone could ever be. When the word *abortion* is mentioned in your presence, don't turn and run. Instead, bow and worship God, your great Redeemer.

When any suggestion of guilt or condemnation comes to your mind, know it is not from God. Don't invite the thought in. Bolt the door of your mind against it, and with every knock on the door, start praising God for His great love and grace.

Turn on praise music and sing!

ACCEPTING THINGS AS THEY ARE

When I was introduced at a summer Bible study being taught at Lake Burton and was asked what brought me to the lake, I said that my friends had loaned me their house and I was writing a book called *When the Hurt Runs Deep.* This connected me with Debbie, a precious gal who is hurting greatly because her momma has advanced Alzheimer's. It's heart wrenching for Debbie to see her mother in this state.

It's been the same for Barbara, my son's mother-in-law, whose husband is afflicted with the condition. Barbara also lost her daughter, my daughter-in-love, in death almost a year ago. How does she make it? She told me she cried and cried and then dried her eyes and, in faith's obedience, let go of the terrible pain. She pulled the plug on all those thoughts about how things should have or could have turned out differently. As a result, she is a comfort and a source of strength, rather than a weight, to her children and grandchildren, and to my son, whom she loves dearly.

How do you live with a hurt like Alzheimer's so that it doesn't absolutely consume you, obliterating the sun with its dark cloud and putting you into deep depression? How do you keep something so devastating from causing you to doubt God's goodness and power?

While there is a natural and healthy stage of mourning that accompanies a loss like this, I think there comes a time when we need to finish our grieving, turn the page, and let the pain go. When will that time come? I believe that God will let you know when that time comes, if you are daily listening for His voice.

It will be a time to release the emotions that can so batter the brain and choose instead to determine that with every thought, every remembrance, we will verbally give thanks always for all things.[6] It will be a new season of life where we recognize that we have done what we can, and there is no more to do. In the final analysis, things are as they are. And what is has been filtered through God's sovereign fingers of love.

In that, we rest our faith.

LETTING GO OF DESTRUCTIVE RELATIONSHIPS

Let me share a portion of an e-mail sent to me by one of my Facebook friends. This woman has suffered twenty-five years of hurt because of her husband's infidelity.

Abraham waited twenty-five years for God to fulfill His covenant promise, and He did. This dear heart has waited twenty-five years for her husband to stop breaking their marriage covenant, and he hasn't.

With every discovery of infidelity, she wrote, "he says he's sorry, vows to change, and plays the part of a repentant husband, father, and Christian — until he is exposed again."

This man has abused drugs and other substances, is addicted to pornography, and is verbally abusive. Yet at the same time, he goes to Sunday school and church and reads the Bible with his wife and grandson every night. Her eight-year-old grandson, whom they are raising, thinks the world of his grandfather.

On the very day she sent me the e-mail, she discovered he had run up a four-hundred-dollar phone bill because of pornography, had reconnected with his drug friends, and was spending a lot of time on the phone with another woman.

She wrote: "I couldn't be in more pain if I were bludgeoned with a baseball bat. I only wish he would just not come home again."

She, of course, would love to be done with "this miserable and lonely life." She's not talking about suicide, just the blessing of going home to be with Jesus. But then there is the grandson to consider, and this godly grandmother fears that "another generation will go down the drain."

She wrote: "I know God is faithful and there must be a reason for this pain. I need to know that there is an end to the turmoil, a place of peace, comfort, and resolve. I feel like a beaten woman. It is extremely hard to forgive over and over, when his actions never change."

Why hasn't she pulled the plug on their marriage and let the source of pain go? "Because," she told me, "I said, 'Till death do us part.' "

However, I believe that with this new discovery about her husband's return to the mire, God is letting her know that biblically she can pull the plug on her marriage and the years of suffering.[7] Please don't think that this ungodly man is a Christian just because he professes to be one. God says, "Do not be deceived" (1 Corinthians 6:9). His habitual lifestyle of sin clearly proves he's not a child of God. First John makes that clear, along with 1 Corinthians 6:9–11; Ephesians 5:3–5; and Galatians 5:19–21.

Briefly, this woman has biblical grounds for divorce. She can, in the eyes of God, terminate her marriage. If, however, she doesn't want a divorce, the teachings of 1 Corinthians 7 tell her how she can live separately from her husband — and perhaps benefit him as he finally sees there is a consequence to his sin. Who knows? He might turn around as Manasseh did!

My point isn't to go into all the biblical ramifications of her marriage and what God says about divorce,[8] but instead to encourage her and others that sometimes we live in hurt *when we don't have to.*

There is a time to pull the plug on a destructive relationship and let the hurt go down the drain.

There is a time to realize that if your child is going to turn around, he or she will have to make the decision.

There is a time to acknowledge that if the alcoholic or drug user is ever going to be healed and set free, he or she will have to make the decision and embrace the truth of Scripture.[9] You can reason, cajole, cry, yell, threaten, plead, beg, or send the person to rehab or counseling. But in the end, he or she is the one who has to make the choice.

There comes a time to pull the plug and give God the opportunity to heal your frazzled emotions.

Some things you cannot fix, beloved, and the One who could didn't — or hasn't. So that's when you ask the Lord if it's time to pull the plug and get on with life.

CHAPTER FIFTEEN:
THE BENEFITS OF SUFFERING

One of my co-workers has a young friend whom she has come to love as a daughter. I met Sharon just last week, and when she heard about the book, she wanted to share her story with me. It came to me as an e-mail:

Quite honestly I don't see that my story is much different than that of many other women. When I think of my hurt, I can't help but think of the thousands of other women who have experienced the same. They remain silent, afraid, and ashamed. They see God through some sick illusion that has been woven through years of hurt and lies. *They don't understand who God really is, or what He freely offers them.* I only offer my story because so many remain silent. And in that silence, they suffer a hurt that penetrates to the depths of their soul.

Ecclesiastes 7:13–14 tells us to "Consider the work of God, for who is able to straighten what He has bent? In the day of prosperity be happy, but in the day of adversity consider — God has made the one as well as the other." Therefore, before I go into Sharon's story, I think it's time for us to look at our pain from a heavenly perspective. Let me share with you seven benefits I can see in the Word of God for hurt that runs deep. As I do, however, let me challenge you to open your Bible and check me out as you consider these conclusions. In fact, check out *everyone* you listen to, and make sure what you hear and embrace as truth lines up with the Word of God.

Before I begin, may I pray with you? I wish I could hold your hand . . .

Father, only You can open the eyes of our understanding, give us eyes to see truth for ourselves, ears to hear it, and hearts to believe. O Father, do this for us. Cup the face of this man, this woman in Your hands and speak to this precious soul face to face. If there is a shadowy veil obscuring his or her spiritual vision, please, in Your mercy and goodness lift the veil so that there is clarity of understanding — and consequently a willingness to believe

251

what You say. I ask this in the name of Your only begotten Son, the Lord Jesus Christ, who sits at Your right hand interceding for this soul who is truly precious to You. Amen.

BENEFIT 1: SUFFERING REVEALS OUR TRUE STATUS

No one wants to be disappointed, run into difficulties, endure stinging defeats, deal with severe trials, or struggle through a time of temptation and testing. Yet strangely enough, times such as these can reveal something important about our lives . . . something we might not have found out any other way.

In fact, our response to suffering tells us a great deal about the real texture of our faith, and our true status with God.

In the gospels of Matthew, Mark, and Luke, you'll find mention of the parable of the sower and the seed. Jesus often used such stories to get His point across to His disciples. Not all people who heard these parables, however, would understand them. The stories were intended for those who truly sought after truth — those who had eyes to see and ears to hear.[1] They contained truths previously hidden but now revealed by the Son of God, the Lord Jesus Christ:

252

mysteries of the kingdom of heaven and mysteries that would help a believer to understand "what on earth" God is doing!

This story of the sower and the seed is an especially important parable, a key to understanding all the other parables Jesus told. Jesus later explained that the seed in the parable represents the Word of God. Through the story, Jesus described what happens when the Word of God is sown in four different places, or soils. He made it clear that He was actually describing the response of four different human hearts.

Three of these soils — hearts — don't get it! Although each responds differently, none of them receive the seed as God intends. As a result, none produce lasting fruit.

One of these soils is the rocky soil — the soil that pertains to our subject. Jesus described it this way:

Others fell on the rocky places, where they did not have much soil; and immediately they sprang up, because they had no depth of soil. But when the sun had risen, they were scorched; and because they had no root, they withered away. (Matthew 13:5–6)

He then explained the picture He had

just painted:

> The one on whom seed was sown on the rocky places, this is the man who hears the word and immediately receives it with joy; yet he has no firm root in himself, but is only temporary, and when affliction or persecution arises because of the word, immediately he falls away. (vv. 20–21)

Do you see why I have referred you to this parable? Jesus specifically mentioned affliction and persecution. The seed in the rocky soil seems to do just fine . . . until the hurt runs deep. When the storm of trials and hardships comes blasting across that rocky soil like a hot, withering wind, it reveals something dramatic about those little seedlings. They have no root, and as a result, they never bear fruit.

What we have here is an individual rocked by adversity. The person can't handle the hurt, and faith can't find a grip in the soil of his heart, because he isn't truly rooted in God. In other words, this person is not a genuine believer, a real Christian.

Now that's something that's very, very important to realize, isn't it? An individual's true status with God never becomes clear until pain crashes into the scene.

If, dear reader, you turn away from God because of your pain, persecution, and suffering, *it shows you are not His child.*

This is the first benefit of suffering.

And yes, I said *benefit.* In fact, it's a benefit beyond calculation!

If you have imagined for years that you were God's child and bound for heaven and then discover that you are not, you have the opportunity to enter into a genuine relationship with the true and living God and live forever with Him. And that, my friend, is as good as it gets!

The willingness to continue believing in the Lord, to continue trusting in Him through a season of great hurt or sorrow, shows you are truly serious about your relationship. Do you remember Job's response to personal tragedy? "Though He slay me, I will hope in Him" (Job 13:15). Although Job became upset with God, he did not cross the line to curse or reject Him. Why? Because Job was a true child of God, a true believer.

If your faith in the Lord has failed the test of suffering, *thank God for that.* I mean those words with all my heart! You now have the opportunity to make things right with Him and get on the right path, the path of hope and blessing. Faith is not faith until it is tested! Only then can you determine whether it's genuine or not.

Hebrews 3:6 tells us we are His house "*if* we hold fast our confidence and the boast of our hope firm until the end." And then, as if God doesn't want us to miss the point, the writer says, "For we have become partakers of Christ, *if* we hold fast the beginning of our assurance firm until the end" (v. 14).

In other words, perseverance is evidence of salvation.

Have you continued to believe, dear one, even though you are struggling with the reason for your pain? If so, it proves your faith is the real thing — genuine! And that's worth celebrating.

BENEFIT 2: SUFFERING DISCIPLINES US

Suffering is a tool God uses to discipline and refine us. Once again, this comes out in the book of Hebrews in the New Testament. Hebrews is a long letter written to a group of people who had suffered greatly and who, in the midst of their suffering, were tempted to turn away from the faith. In their great sorrow and distress, some were tempted to stop listening to God — to go back to the comfort and security of their former worship and quit identifying with Jesus Christ. Perhaps you relate to this because you've experienced nothing but pain and rejection since you let it be known that you've become a follower of Jesus Christ.

The writer of Hebrews tells those discouraged by suffering to fix their eyes on Jesus and keep in mind what He suffered on their behalf. God will not take you where His Son has not been! Jesus learned obedience through the things He suffered, although He was the Son of God.[2]

Having affirmed that, he then wrote the following in Hebrews 12:5–14. Read it carefully, and then we'll discuss it. (How I wish it could be a two-sided discussion. This is such a wonderful passage!) As you read, underline every reference to *the child of God: son, you, us.* This is for you . . . today.

"My son, do not regard lightly the discipline of the Lord, nor faint when you are reproved by Him; for those whom the Lord loves He disciplines, and He scourges every son whom He receives." It is for discipline that you endure; God deals with you as with sons; for what son is there whom his father does not discipline? But if you are without discipline, *of which all have become partakers,* then you are illegitimate children and not sons. Furthermore, we had earthly fathers to discipline us, and we respected them; shall we not much rather be subject to the Father of spirits, and live? For they disciplined us for a short time as seemed best to them, but He disciplines us for our good, so that we may share His holiness. All discipline for the moment seems not to be joyful, but sorrowful; yet to those who have been trained by it, afterwards it yields the peaceful fruit of righteousness.

Therefore, strengthen the hands that are weak and the knees that are feeble, and make straight paths for your feet, so that the limb which is lame may not be put out of joint, but rather be healed.

Pursue peace with all men, and the sanctification without which no one will see the Lord.

It's clear, isn't it? Discipline proves we are truly His kids! Because God is our Father and He wants us to be all we should be, He disciplines us. The Greek word for "discipline" is *paideia,* which means "to train," as you would a child. Just as you disciplined your children (and if you didn't, you should have — and probably wish you had), so God disciples or trains us. And guess what? It wasn't fun when your earthly father did it, and it's not fun with God! Discipline is never joyous, but it is good. It brings righteousness — and with it peace. Oh, the awesome peace that comes when you know you are right with God. Right with God and becoming more like God! The purpose of discipline is so we'll be more godly, more "godlike." We are to be holy even as He is holy in all our behavior, which is what God tells us in 1 Peter 1:15–16.

God disciplined Moses, and it wasn't easy for Moses. Moses asked God more than once to allow him to take the children of Israel across the Jordan into the Promised Land, and God said no. Moses died on the wrong side of the Jordan because he did not do as God said; Moses didn't treat God as holy. God had told him to speak to the rock in front of all the people, and it would bring forth water. Moses was so irritated at the people who were murmuring about thirst that, instead of speaking to the rock, he *hit* it with his staff. Twice!

Part of the reason Moses' tantrum was such an offense to God can be better understood when we read 1 Corinthians 10, where Paul tells us that the rock was Christ.[3] Moses had waited eighty years to cross the

Jordan and then — so near his goal — he blew it in a flash of temper and disrespect. At the end of his life, however, Moses had nothing but praise and honor for the Rock of Israel. He taught Israel to sing a song that included these lyrics: "The Rock! His work is perfect, for all His ways are just; a God of faithfulness and without injustice, righteous and upright is He" (Deuteronomy 32:4).

God disciplined King David fourfold for his sin with Bathsheba, yet David proclaimed God blameless when He judges.[4] When David numbered the children of Israel in violation of God's explicit instruction, God disciplined him, sending pestilence on Israel. Seventy thousand men died. Rather than being angry at God, railing at Him, David stopped the plague by building an altar and presenting God with a burnt offering.[5] And how did God describe David in the New Testament? As a man after His heart![6] The discipline of suffering works within us when we accept it and respond in a way that is pleasing to God.

The apostle Paul was given a thorn in the flesh to discipline him, to keep him from exalting himself because of what he had seen when God caught him up to the third heaven. Although Paul pled with God three times to take away that hurtful, distressing thorn, He didn't! And yet what did Paul say in his final epistle? He declared God the righteous Judge:

> For I am already being poured out as a drink offering, and the time of my departure has come. I have fought the good fight, I have finished the course, I have kept the faith; in the future there is laid up for me the crown of righteousness, which the Lord, the righteous Judge, will award to me on that day; and not only to me, but also to all who have loved His appearing. . . . The Lord will rescue me from every evil deed, and will bring me safely to His heavenly kingdom; to Him be the glory forever and ever. Amen. (2 Timothy 4:6–8, 18)

What will you say about God in the midst of your discipline, your "child training"? Don't walk away like a petulant child, slamming the door, murmuring under your breath. Honor your heavenly Father. Remember, once the sting of the divine woodshed experience is past, the discipline yields the peaceable fruit of righteousness. Peace is coming! You're going to be more like Jesus! Sing Moses' song. Pray David's

261

prayer. Like Paul, look to the reward to come.

BENEFIT 3: SUFFERING LOOSENS THE WORLD'S GRIP ON US

Hurt weans us from this world and the things of this world. It makes the prospect of heaven sweeter.

The simple fact is, we live in a world of hurt, and though we may experience good seasons of healing and joy in our lives, the pains of earth will never go away on this side of heaven.

This is the consequence of the choice of our first father and mother: Adam and Eve. Choosing to disobey God, they listened to the smooth voice of the serpent and sought the benefit of knowing good and evil for themselves. They were convinced they could handle independence from God, becoming like God, knowing good and evil. To say it didn't work has to be the understatement of all time.

We suffer because we experientially know evil. It is a consequence of Adam and Eve's disobedience, their desiring what God had forbidden: the fruit of the tree of the knowledge of good and evil. In Adam, we chose to know evil, and we will experience it until Jesus returns, binds Satan, casts him into the bottomless pit, and brings His own glorious dominion to earth.

Stop and think about all those who knew God but who wished to die — or wished they had never have been born. Don't ever imagine you're "all alone." Others have been where you are. Your tears are not stored in a bottle alone; they are mingled with those of the saints of the ages.[7] The fact is, life is often hard and disappointing because of sin, suffering, and conflict.

Job wanted to die.[8]

Elijah wanted to die.[9]

Jeremiah wanted to die.[10]

David, the writer of many psalms, wrote longingly of God's presence and of dwelling in the house of the Lord forever.

Paul longed to be clothed with his body from heaven, knowing that to be absent from the body was to be present with the Lord.[11] He viewed death as much better than living on in this world, because he knew about heaven.[12] His unnamed thorn in the flesh would be forever gone, and he would leave behind all the brand marks he bore on his body as a result of following Christ.[13]

Oh dear one . . . can you look at your "brandmarks" — the scars of your suffering, both seen and unseen — that way? It will turn your scars into trophies.

And what about the "things," the stuff of the world? Has your suffering changed your focus, your priorities, your driving desire and ambition? What's really important to you in life now?

Times of suffering have a way of putting questions like that into perspective.

James, a highly successful, self-sufficient businessman — the husband of a dear friend — had his life put in perspective when he was diagnosed with cancer. It was the first thing he couldn't fix himself, and his hurt went very, very deep.

But it brought him to Jesus! And from that time, life took a radical 180-degree turn. The diagnosis of death not only brought eternal life but also brought a new view of what was really important. Material possessions, pleasure, and prestige lost their grip. James couldn't believe he had been so blind.

His story reminds me of what Paul wrote from prison in his epistle of joy:

But whatever things were gain to me, those things I have counted as loss for the sake of Christ. More than that, I count all things to be loss in view of the surpassing value of knowing Christ Jesus my Lord, for whom I have suffered the loss of all things, and count them but rubbish so that I may gain Christ, and may be found in Him, not having a righteousness of my own derived from the Law, but that which is through faith in Christ, the righteousness which comes from God on the basis of faith, that I may know Him and the power of His resurrection and the fellowship of His sufferings, being conformed to His death; in order that I may attain to the resurrection from the dead. (Philippians 3:7–11)

And where do you stand when it comes to the things, the stuff of the world? Has your suffering changed your focus? Has deep-running hurt moved you to look at your life and priorities in a new way? What's important now? Is it less of earth and more of heaven?

If so, you're experiencing a priceless benefit.

BENEFIT 4: WE LEARN THE VALUE OF LISTENING TO GOD

Before we explore this fourth benefit, let me make it clear that suffering isn't always a consequence of our behavior. If pain crashes into our lives, we can't automatically assume it's because we have sinned or failed in some way. Be very careful of thinking *this* happened to you because you're just not a good person or that you "don't deserve any better."

Some who have been misused, abused, or beaten to a pulp think it's because they somehow deserve it; they're convinced they must have done something wrong or people wouldn't treat them this way. They must be bad!

This is the favorite line of abusers, and it's a lie straight from the pit of hell.

All hurt is not deserved or earned.

All suffering is not of our making.

Hurt comes because of where we live — within a culture and among a people who have refused Jesus and turned their backs on God. We live, as Paul wrote, in the midst of a crooked and perverse generation. Our world is in the shape it is today because of the evil of man: his rebellion against God and his distortions of God, the people of God, and the Word of God. (How often do we see it in movies or on television?)

Now, having said this, we need to see the other side of the coin of hurt: sometimes suffering *is* the consequence of our choices.

There are times when we simply insist on our own, self-centered way, instead of seeking God's way, God's heart, and God's wise choices for our lives. And what we want — what we feel we simply must have to be happy, satisfied, or complete — may not be what God wants for us at all.

So we make wrong choices, and then we must endure the consequences of those wrong choices.

Speaking of Israel, God says, "They soon forgat his works; they waited not for his counsel: but lusted exceedingly in the wilderness, and tempted God in the desert. And he gave them their request; but sent leanness into their soul" (Psalm 106:13–15, KJV).

They just had to have their way. And they got it — punishment and affliction seven times over, just as God warned them repeatedly in Leviticus 26!

Have you suffered (even in your conscience) because you had to have your way — you had to have that man, that woman, that promotion, that possession, that approbation, that whatever? You knew your desire didn't line up with the Word of God, the will of God, or the character of God, but that didn't stop you. You went for it and got it.

Now you're hurting, aren't you? Hurting deep. Maybe tormented in your heart.

Overcome by a guilty conscience. You're suffering — and you have to live with the consequences!

So what did you learn? Whatever lesson you've learned, whatever truth you've now grasped hold of is your "benefit" from suffering. It's a lousy way to get the benefit, but if it keeps you from more wrong choices and drives you into a deeper relationship with God, then it is worth it. It really is. The psalmist wrote, "Before I was afflicted I went astray, but now I keep Your word. . . . It is good for me that I was afflicted, that I may learn Your statutes" (119:67, 71).

When you study the Old Testament, it becomes patently obvious that Israel's hurt ran deep because of their rebellion against God and their stiff-necked refusal to listen to Him. If you were to read through the Old Testament prophets and mark every reference to "listen," the truth would come home full force: the evil came because they did not listen to God. They thought they could "take a vacation" from God's righteous standards. They thought they could get away with disobedience. They could not. And neither can you or I.

God wrote it in His book: "Be sure your sin will find you out" (Numbers 32:23) and "The one who sows to his own flesh will from the flesh reap corruption" (Galatians 6:8).

Yet throughout the Old Testament you see His grace, His goodness, His mercy, His *hesed* (loving-kindness). God hasn't rejected His covenant people, Israel, and He won't. Israel will be restored.[14] Messiah will rule in Jerusalem. When Messiah comes, Zechariah tells us, they will "look on Me whom they have pierced; and they will mourn for Him, as one mourns for an only son, and they will weep bitterly over Him like the bitter weeping over a firstborn" (Zechariah 12:10).

They will realize that most of their suffering came because they wouldn't believe God. They stumbled because the One they rejected was the cornerstone.

When the hurt is of your own making you need to thank God that He is righteous, just, and equitable — then dry your tears. Accept the consequences of your sin. "Strengthen the hands that are weak and the knees that are feeble, and make straight paths for your feet, so that the limb which is lame may not be put out of joint, but rather be healed" (Hebrews 12:12–13). Be healed and pursue holiness.

Therefore, since Christ has suffered in

the flesh, arm yourselves also with the same purpose, because he who has suffered in the flesh has ceased from sin, so as to live the rest of the time in the flesh no longer for the lusts of men, but for the will of God. For the time already past is sufficient for you to have carried out the desire of the Gentiles, having pursued a course of sensuality, lusts, drunkenness, carousing, drinking parties and abominable idolatries. (1 Peter 4:1–3)

BENEFIT 5: SUFFERING CAN ADVANCE GOD'S PURPOSE IN YOUR LIFE

Have you ever considered that the hurt you suffer in your life — whether physical or emotional — might be for God's glory or used to achieve His purpose? Instead of fighting your affliction or running from it or trying to wallpaper over it, you can choose to submit to God's sovereignty in your life. When you do, watch how God uses your current circumstances to display the sufficiency and power of His grace.

Do you remember when God called Moses to be His designated spokesman, to stand before Pharaoh and lead the children of Israel out of Egypt? Moses was not a man to whom words came easily. He was unskilled in speech, never eloquent.[15] He described himself as "slow of speech and slow of tongue" (Exodus 4:10). And what was God's response?

> The LORD said to him, "Who has made man's mouth? Or who makes him mute or deaf, or seeing or blind? Is it not I, the LORD? Now then go, and I, even I, will be with your mouth, and teach you what you are to say." (vv. 11–12)

First, notice that God didn't contradict Moses' self-evaluation. He didn't say, "Oh, come on, Moses, it's not as bad as you think. All you need is a little practice." No, what God told Moses was that He Himself was behind those limitations and had a purpose for allowing them. There is a purpose in everything that God allows.

Second, God assured Moses that He would be with him in spite of those limitations. God would compensate for his "deficiency." He would accomplish His perfect purpose through this imperfect man. The fact is, God works through our limitations and difficult circumstances to show us that He is God and that He is sufficient for our every need! As He says in Hebrews 13:5, He will never leave us or forsake us. As He has purposed so it will come to pass; what God plans no man can thwart.[16]

Remember the man born blind whom Jesus healed on the temple mount? When Jesus' disciples asked, "Rabbi, who sinned, this man or his parents, that he would be born blind?" Jesus answered, "It was neither that this man sinned, nor his parents; but it was so that the works of God might be displayed in him" (John 9:2–3).

The apostle Paul was given a thorn in the flesh, "a messenger of Satan" to torment him. When he asked God for the third time to remove it, God said no.[17] We've talked about this already, so why do I bring it up again? Because this time I want you to see the *reason* for the thorn. The thorn was to keep Paul from exalting himself. And why would he do that? Because of the revelations he had experienced when he was caught up into paradise and shown marvelous things that he wasn't to speak about. Paul's thorn would keep him from the awful sin of pride.

And what would God do to compensate for the thorn?

He would let Paul experience the power and sufficiency of His grace!

Paul's response is our example: "Therefore I am well content with weaknesses, with insults, with distresses, with persecutions, with difficulties, for Christ's sake; for when I am weak, then I am strong" (2 Corinthians 12:10).

If God chooses to allow suffering to enter your experience in order to advance His purposes in Your life and give you a deeper experience of Him, the worst thing you could do would be to react in anger and bitterness.

By doing so, you are essentially saying, "God, I don't want Your plan for my life. If I have to endure this heartache, then I don't want You to advance Your purposes in me. I don't want Your provision of extra grace and the sense of Your nearness, because the price is too high!"

Perhaps God has reined you in through some physical infirmity so that the two of you can spend more time together. In response you might argue with God, get angry and stay angry, walk away in rebellion, or seek some temporary, artificial way to nullify the hurt or make it go away. But none of those things will bring healing, and none will help you move on in life.

Your other option — the best option — is to submit to His wise sovereignty and watch how God uses your situation to display the sufficiency and power of His grace.

Most of us tend to be so focused on our body, on our appearance, and our physical well-being, that it brings us great distress when we don't "measure up" in our own eyes, or in the eyes of others.

I think of Joan and her husband, Dick, who in addition to being medical missionaries to India, have also been faithful Precept Ministries students and supporters for many years. I'll let Joan describe what is happening to her body, the hurt it brings, and how she deals with it.

My back is bending forward toward the ground. It is unmistakable and cannot be ignored. I try to smile extra and make people comfortable.

I grew up with a cerebral palsy twin brother and have always known the quick ignoring glances and "look-aways" that come over some people. Some people will make an attempt and give some kind of smile, but very few people actually seem comfortable with the situation, unless they have known me for a long time.

One friend is embarrassed to be seen with me and has told me so. The unrelenting physical pain and limitations are bad enough, but this is another problem that is compounding the hurt. Extra pain comes with unknowing or uncaring people adding to an already changing landscape for me.

Christians could be such a tool in God's hands if they were made more aware of those who are different from themselves. When someone wants to know how I feel . . . I can answer, "I have a weaker and weakening body, but oh, I am stronger in the Lord!"

And so she is.

Joan realizes only too well that, unless the Lord intervenes, this is a hurt that will continue to worsen as the months and years go by. In situations like these, our suffering serves to remind us and those around us of God's purposes and perspective: the Lord "does not delight in the strength of the horse; He does not take pleasure in the legs of a man. The LORD favors those who fear Him, those who wait for His lovingkindness" (Psalm 147:10–11).

We are a culture that likes, admires, and follows "beautiful people" — many times without considering where they are headed. Jesus, the Son of God, was not a show-stopper! Isaiah tells us what Messiah would look like and how people would respond to Him:

> He has no stately form or majesty
>> that we should look upon Him,
>> nor appearance that we should be attracted to Him.
> He was despised and forsaken of men,
>> a man of sorrows and acquainted with grief;
> and like one from whom men hide their face
> He was despised, and we did not esteem Him. (53:2–3)

Paul, the apostle, was also denigrated for his appearance. The word was, "his letters are weighty and strong, but his personal presence is unimpressive and his speech contemptible" (2 Corinthians 10:10).

In addition to his personal appearance and unpolished speech, there was that distressing "thorn in the flesh" we've already discussed. Some who have put all the pieces together about Paul's life believe his thorn in the flesh was an eye condition that made him rather repulsive to look at. Yet from all you know about Jesus and Paul (and the little bit you know about Joan), wouldn't you want to be around them and spend time with them no matter how they looked?

Who a person is on the inside matters a great deal more than a temporary physical beauty that will only fade with each passing day. Suffering reminds us that God's purposes are accomplished not because of our beauty or strength or influence, but because of "the surpassing greatness of His power toward us who believe" (Ephesians 1:19).

If you submit to His purposes in your life, He will begin to restore and rebuild you from the inside out. We are men and women who were born with a distorted image of His likeness, and it's the mission of God's Word and God's Spirit in our lives to transform us into the image of God's own Son.

BENEFIT 6: SUFFERING BRINGS US TO TOTAL DEPENDENCE ON GOD

Deep, exhausting, unrelenting, unrelieved hurt can bring you to the end of yourself.

And that's the very best place to be.

Complete brokenness often brings total dependence on God, which gives anyone with deep hurts their best chance of healing and recovery.

Let's return to Sharon, whom you met briefly at the start of this chapter. She wanted me to share her story in the hopes that it would help others who suffer deeply.

My story must begin with my mother. I'm confident that when she chose to marry and have children, she intended to be the best mother and wife she could be. She had no way of knowing that at the age of twenty-four her husband would die and she would be left with three small children. I was five years old at the time, and the oldest. Mother's life changed on that fateful day, and things would be very dark for a very long time.

Sharon watched helplessly as her mother spiraled out of control, even attempting to take her own life on several occasions. With her mother unable to offer love or security, this young girl became the victim of several male relatives who abused her over the course of several years. You can imagine the hurt and shame that haunted her life during that time. "I lost my innocence, self-worth, and hope and was left feeling unloved and unwanted."

Praise God, this young woman came to faith in Christ as a teenager. But she still couldn't move beyond the pain of her dark past.

I wanted to believe God could really forgive and forget the evil I felt that lived inside me. I wanted to believe that He could love me the way He loved other "good" girls. But deep inside, far hidden from anyone, I kept the lies alive. Lies that said, no matter how hard I tried, I would never be whole, free, good, or pure again. I would never be loved or feel secure. . . .

As soon as I thought there was healing, the hurt would rise up within me again.

Have you been there, my friend, wondering if the ache would ever go away? Listen to what happened next and take hope! Finally, she explained,

God would use a series of events that would cause me to fall flat on my face before Him, begging for something more. I wasn't sure I knew what I was asking for, but I just knew there had to be more than this existence of constant emotional pain. If what I had read and studied in God's word was true, if everything I learned about God through doing the *Lord* series[18] was truth, then I had to search for the God of the Bible and not the God I had come to believe in.

"Flat on my face."

Any hurt that brings you there, beloved, so that you "then . . . search for the God of the Bible and not the God I had come to believe in" is worth it. It's worth a world of hurt, because this world is passing away. God is about to shake the things that can be shaken, so that those that cannot be shaken will be seen for what they are.[19]

HEALING TRUTH #11

Deep, exhausting, unrelenting hurt can
bring you to the end of yourself —
to complete and total dependence
on God — which is the best place
you could ever be.

I want you to think about this next statement, because it may be one of the most important sentences in this entire book: *Whatever it takes to get you to the place where God is your all in all and you live in total dependence on Him is worth the pain.*

Let's see how it worked in Sharon's life. I feel like she is my spiritual daughter because she came to me through learning to study

280

Since then God has been gently sharing with me the truth of His words. The turning point was when a dear friend shared with me that God calls me His beloved. It says it in God's Word! I had never seen it written by God before! He calls me His beloved, I am holy and precious in His sight — these are truths I now cling to. They are truths that have replaced the lies and hurt of a child. . . .

It is in the journey of plunging into the depths of God's Word and getting to know the heart of God that has given me hope, security, and love. As I have learned to study for myself, God has created in my heart a hunger to know Him, and it's in the knowing Him that there has been healing.

Sharon's words echo the truth the apostle Paul discovered in his own world of hurt. When He first saved him, God told Paul he would suffer great things. All of this came home to me in a fresh way when I wrote the book *Lord, Give Me a Heart for You,* a study on 2 Corinthians — a letter in which Paul bares his soul as nowhere else in all his writings. When some of those in the church in Corinth began to demean him in a variety of ways, putting down him as a man and as an apostle, Paul — under divine inspiration — responded in 2 Corinthians 11:23–30 with these words:

Are they servants of Christ? — I speak as if insane — I more so; in far more labors, in far more imprisonments, beaten times without number, often in danger of death. Five times I received from the Jews thirty-nine lashes. Three times I was beaten with rods, once I was stoned, three times I was shipwrecked, a night and a day I have spent in the deep.

I have been on frequent journeys, in dangers from rivers, dangers from robbers, dangers from my countrymen, dangers from the Gentiles, dangers in the city, dangers in the wilderness, dangers on the sea, dangers among false brethren; I have been in labor and hardship, through many sleepless nights, in hunger and thirst, often without food, in cold and exposure.

Apart from such external things, there is the daily pressure on me of concern for all the churches. Who is weak without my being weak? Who is led into sin without my intense concern?

If I have to boast, I will boast of what pertains to my weakness.

It's weakness that brings us flat on our face and puts our eyes on eternity. Read the following words thoughtfully:

But we have this treasure in earthen vessels, so that the surpassing greatness of the power will be of God and not from ourselves; we are afflicted in every way, but not crushed; perplexed, but not despairing; persecuted, but not forsaken; struck down, but not destroyed; always carrying about in the body the dying of Jesus, so that the life of Jesus also may be manifested in our body. (2 Corinthians 4:7–10)

Afflicted . . . perplexed . . . persecuted . . . struck down. Have you experienced any of the hurts Paul described in this passage? God wants you to understand that there is a divine purpose in it all, no matter how painful. Listen to Paul's next words:

For we who live are constantly being delivered over to death for Jesus' sake, so that the life of Jesus also may be manifested in our mortal flesh. (v. 11)

This is what Paul meant when he said, "It is no longer I who live, but Christ lives in me" (Galatians 2:20). It's one of the ways we are brought flat on our faces. And yet even in our total impotence (as strange as it might seem), others who are observing our lives can sometimes catch a glimpse of God's supernatural power! Watch Paul's next statement: "So death works in us, but life in you" (2 Corinthians 4:12).

BENEFIT 7: SUFFERING EQUIPS US TO HELP OTHERS IN THEIR HURT

Your hurt, when handled biblically, serves as your training ground for ministry — often for ministry in the very arena where you have suffered.

It's eye-opening to consider all the ministries and charities that have been launched as a result of hurt that has run deep. Dick Mason, the current chairman of the board of directors at Precept Ministries International, has a severely autistic grandson. Talk about heartbreak and unrelenting pain! I can't even begin to imagine the hurt Dick's son and daughter-in-law face each day in caring for their autistic child.

Recent statistics show that one out of every one hundred children in the United States has an autism-spectrum disorder.

From the moment of diagnosis, life is never the same for their parents. The majority of marriages do not survive the incredible stress of providing 24/7 care for these precious but challenging children.

Instead of letting the hurt tear them apart, Dave and Krista took their pain to God and asked for His direction. At His leading, they founded Benjamin's Hope, a facility and ministry designed to provide practical support to parents of children with developmental disabilities — including a safe place for their child while they get away for a needed time of rest and respite.

Caring for Ben is their lot, an unexpected bend in their road. It's an enormous responsibility that our sovereign God has allowed in their life for a greater and, until recently, unseen purpose. And instead of rebelling, instead of becoming angry and bitter, instead of repeating, "Why us? Why us?" they have bowed the knee, submitted to God, and asked, "What would you have us to do?"

Beloved, let me speak a word here on behalf of surrender.

There is something beautiful about submitting to the God who loves you and longs for your best. Is it easy? No, perhaps not. Not at first. But after a moment or two, oh, how glad you will be that you bowed your knee to the Lord Jesus. Just to feel the warm shafts of light on your bowed back . . . and to watch them pierce the darkness of disappointment. So very slowly, or sometimes all at once, you begin to see the outlines of His plan, and how He will use your hurt to help the hurting.

The back cover of Ed Underwood's book *When God Breaks Your Heart* has this question: "Why is God letting this happen to me?"

Sound familiar? It's a normal question and certainly not one God faults us for. Instead, He uses that heart-wrenching question to drive us to Himself, where we rest by faith, even if we don't get an answer.

God gave Ed a significant platform as the pastor of the historic Church of the Open Door in California. But then came the diagnosis of lymphoma, a disease of such excruciating pain that many sufferers choose suicide as a means of escape. In the throes of unbearable agony Ed planned his own death — until he contemplated the benefit of living through the pain. His decision to live in the power of God has been used by God to minister to countless people who also deal with unrelenting pain.

Ed's sorrows have not been wasted; they

have been *redeemed,* because his pain became his platform for ministry, just as God intended and purposed. Ed's book is an excellent source of comfort when you think you "just can't take anymore."

Your hurt, in its many varied forms, isn't just about you, beloved. It has a far greater purpose. Listen:

> For all things are for your sakes, so that the grace which is spreading to more and more people may cause the giving of thanks to abound to the glory of God.
>
> Therefore we do not lose heart, but though our outer man is decaying, yet our inner man is being renewed day by day. For momentary, light affliction is producing for us an eternal weight of glory far beyond all comparison. (2 Corinthians 4:15–17)

Did you notice how Paul described the hurt as "momentary, light affliction"? How could he say such a thing, after all the trials, troubles, and tribulations he endured? Oh, if only we, too, could look at our hurts this way!

How did Paul manage it? Read the verse that follows:

. . . While we look not at the things which are seen, but at the things which are not seen; for the things which are seen are temporal, but the things which are not seen are eternal. (v. 18)

It's a matter of focus. A matter of keeping your eyes on Jesus. As Hebrews 12:2 says, "fixing our eyes on Jesus . . . who for the joy set before Him endured the cross, despising the shame, and has sat down at the right hand of the throne of God." Jesus went from the cross of earth to the right hand of God in heaven, His purpose complete and fulfilled.

Because of sin, Jesus had to bear the cross before He could wear the crown. In the same way, He calls on you and me to deny ourselves, take up our cross, and follow Him. In so doing, we will save our lives.[20]

Our lives will have eternal value and everlasting significance, and someday all the hurt and darkness life brings will be gone forever and ever. We will live in a city that "has no need of the sun or of the moon to shine on it, for the glory of God has illumined it, and its lamp is the Lamb" (Revelation 21:23).

Our focus must be the eternal! That is the way you endure the cross that comes before the crown.

This life is temporal. The hurt is temporal. It has an end. And what a beginning it leads to!

O God, stamp eternity upon our eyes.

CHAPTER SIXTEEN:
THE HURT YET TO COME

Our nation's magnificent Declaration of Independence speaks of certain unalienable rights, such as life, liberty, and the pursuit of happiness.

We ought to be free to pursue happiness.

But we can't turn that pursuit into an *entitlement*.

Some people who find themselves in the midst of personal suffering feel cheated. "Don't I deserve to be happy?" they ask. Sometimes Christians ask a similar question: *"Doesn't God want me to be happy?"* We have accepted the premise that faith in Jesus and a destination of heaven ought to somehow shield us from disappointment and heartache.

But that's not what Scripture promises.

The Bible promises peace to those who trust their lives to the care of Jesus and an ultimate working-together-for-good for those who love Him and who are called according to His purposes.[1]

But God never promised a hassle-free, pain-free life. Not on this side of heaven!

Christians in repressive countries around the world understand what it means to suffer for their faith, knowing that they could be put to death simply for possessing a Bible or for mentioning the name of Jesus.

Thus far, we Christians have experienced very little suffering in the United States for our faith in Christ. But it could very well come. And sooner than many of us may expect.

I firmly believe that our identification with Jesus Christ and our allegiance to Him *will* be tested, and tested to the limit, just as has happened in so many other nations around the world.

Never mind all the current political issues — red state, blue state, Republican, Democrat, Independent, whatever. For the moment, just focus on this: are we prepared for the time when the hurt of the cross runs earthquake deep in our nation?

Yes, of course, we Christians through the years have known the hurt of being ridiculed because of our faith and because of the lifestyle changes our convictions have prompted. Husbands, wives, parents, and children have experienced loneliness and rejection as they have placed loyalty to Jesus even higher than loyalty to blood ties or old friendships. Men and women have certainly lost jobs, offices, and positions of responsibility for refusing to compromise on a host of moral and ethical issues.

We've been the brunt of jokes and the object of disdain in our homes and families, in our schools, and in our places of business. But it usually hasn't gone much further than that.

Not yet.

But what if we woke up tomorrow to realize that Christians — authentic, Bible-believing, Christ-followers — had been labeled the enemy of society? What if it was suddenly deemed a "hate crime" to tell others that Jesus is the only way to God? Are we really so far from such a day?

One thing these past couple of years should have taught all of us is that when change happens, it can take place with shocking speed. Many of us look back on the past year and wonder, "How in the world could all of these changes — negative and harmful changes — have taken place in our beloved nation in just a few short months?"

I don't want any of us to be caught unaware — surprised and shocked — about the days that are upon us. We could very well be entering a time in our nation when a new kind of hurt will run deeper than we had ever imagined. In God's Word, it's called "the fellowship of His sufferings."[2] *Fellowship* means "to share in common." We are to share in the sufferings that continue in the body, the church, of Jesus Christ — sufferings that come from uncompromising righteousness.

Let's take a closer look at what this means.

LIFE'S THREE PRIORITIES

In the past few decades, many voices within America's Christian media have focused on *material prosperity.* As children of the King, we're told, we deserve royal treatment. The best of the best, in this life and the next! These prosperity teachers have forgotten (or ignored) that our primary calling as believers in Jesus Christ is to a cross. And what does a cross bring? Separation, suffering, and persecution. I'm speaking here of a deep-running hurt . . . that in the days to come could lead directly to martyrdom. (The martyrdom that the first apostles experienced. Martyrdom as multitudes around the world are experiencing in greater numbers than in all the centuries past!)

Why should that shock us? Why should

we be blindsided by suffering?

Remember what Peter said to persecuted saints in the first century?

> Beloved, do not be surprised at the fiery ordeal among you, which comes upon you for your testing, *as though some strange thing were happening to you.* (1 Peter 4:12)

It's *not* strange, and it *shouldn't* surprise us.

Paul wrote to the church at Philippi and reminded them: "For to you it has been granted for Christ's sake, not only to believe in Him, but also to suffer for His sake, experiencing the same conflict which you saw in me, and now hear to be in me" (Philippians 1:29–30).

Paul had experienced it, *and so would they.* Suffering is in the job description of every child of God. In the same New Testament letter, Paul wrote of his passion "that I may know Him and the power of His resurrection and the fellowship of His sufferings . . ." (3:10). As I noted earlier, the word for "fellowship" — *koinonia* — means "to share in common." Oh, that this would be our passion — a passion that would keep us strong and courageous, especially in the days that are coming in America.

Jesus didn't promise His followers a crown in this life. That was never God's plan (and He makes this clear from the beginning of the Bible). Listen to what He said to the multitude who were fascinated by His miracles and the free lunches of fish and bread. Read Mark 8:34–38 aloud and remember, these are the very words of Jesus Himself.

And He summoned the crowd with His disciples, and said to them, "If anyone wishes to come after Me, he must deny himself, and take up his cross and follow Me. For whoever wishes to save his life will lose it, but whoever loses his life for My sake and the gospel's will save it. For what does it profit a man to gain the whole world, and forfeit his soul? For what will a man give in exchange for his soul? For whoever is ashamed of Me and My words in this adulterous and sinful generation, the Son of Man will also be ashamed of him when He comes in the glory of His Father with the holy angels."

Did you see the first three things Jesus asks us to do? I would number those with my pencil in the text so I wouldn't miss them.

"If anyone wishes to come after Me, he must . . .

. . . deny himself

. . . take up his cross

. . . and follow Me."

This is what it takes to be a follower, or disciple, of Jesus Christ.

First, I must deny myself.

Can you think of any statement that runs more cross-grained to our culture than *that?* It doesn't sound much like "prosperity theology," does it?

Second, I am to take up my cross!

"A cross?" someone might say. "Oh, I have a lovely fourteen-karat gold one with pearls that my grandmother gave me." Or maybe, "I have a rugged wooden one from my dad. I think it was from his hippie days."

No, that's not what Jesus had in mind. All kinds of people wear crosses around their necks these days, including people who don't believe in Jesus at all or profess any allegiance to Him.

Jesus, however, was not about jewelry. In fact, if you had been standing in the crowd at the moment when Jesus made that statement about the cross, you would have heard an audible gasp from those around you. A *cross?* How cruel! How offensive!

In that day, the cross was an instrument of death — a slow and torturous execution device, something so ignominious and terrible that no Roman citizen would ever have to die that way. Crosses lined the roads of countries Rome conquered, so all would see the horrific fate of those who went against Roman law.

Having a gold cross around your neck, then, is really like having a golden electric chair or a sterling silver hangman's noose. The cross is an instrument of execution! Of death!

Jesus called His followers to actually die to self. How strange that sounds in a culture where it is all about *ME,* where so many believe that we are supposed to "look out for number one."

Which brings us to the third thing: Jesus says, "Follow Me."

When Jesus said "follow," He used the word in its present tense, which means it is to be your lifestyle, a continuous habit of life with no vacations from God or sabbaticals to do as *you* please.

The summary of those three things can be seen in the very next verse: "For whoever wishes to save his life will lose it, but whoever loses his life for My sake and the gospel's will save it" (v. 35).

Jesus was calling those who would be His disciples to lose their lives in Him and in His mission. And what is that mission? Spreading everywhere the great good news that the death, burial, and resurrection of Jesus Christ brings forgiveness of sins and eternal life. You see it repeated again and again in many ways, right through to the end of the New Testament in the closing verses of the book of Revelation.

So what was the conclusion of Jesus' words to the multitudes who were following Him out of curiosity, fascination, or a simple desire to see what He was all about? Let's read it again:

For what does it profit a man to gain the whole world, and forfeit his soul? For what will a man give in exchange for his soul? For whoever is ashamed of Me and My words in this adulterous and sinful generation, the Son of Man will also be ashamed of him when He comes in the glory of His Father with the holy angels. (vv. 36–38)

Most men and women today seek whatever they can grab out of life. But whatever portion they may come up with in their tightly clenched fingers, if they don't have Jesus, they will forfeit their own souls.

The only way to escape this terrible second death is through the cross, where He laid down His life to purchase yours. But know this, dear reader: it will not be without hurt — often costly, deep-reaching hurt. Becoming a Christian often means sharp relational pain, because it divides you from family or friends and takes you on a different road, a narrow road. But it is a sweet hurt, because it is the fellowship of His sufferings. "For just as the sufferings of Christ are ours in abundance, so also our comfort is abundant through Christ" (2 Corinthians 1:5).

THE HIGH COST OF DISCIPLESHIP

As you read the gospel accounts, you'll find this matter of laying down one's life is not an isolated topic. Jesus makes it clear over and over what it takes to be His disciple.

In Mark 10, we have the account of a young man who owned a great deal of property and pursued Jesus because he wanted to know how he could inherit eternal life. As Jesus spoke to him, putting His finger directly on the young man's obsession with possessions, we read that "Looking at him, Jesus felt a love for him" (v. 21).

Yet despite the love Jesus felt for him, He could not give this man eternal life, because his possessions were his life. After the young man sadly walked off into the distance, Jesus declared, "How hard it will be for those who are wealthy to enter the kingdom of God!" And then Jesus said it again, addressing his disciples, "Children, how hard it is to enter the kingdom of God!" (vv. 23–24)

It is hard, beloved, because it calls us to deny ourselves and take up our cross and follow Him.

Our love of Jesus must be supreme, and that can cost us the hurt of separation from those closest to us — including our family. If you have experienced something like that, then you know what I'm talking about, don't you? Sometimes our relatives or friends just plain don't like real Christianity. As a result, we may find ourselves excluded from family events, celebrations, vacations, and weddings. And holidays? Well, we may find ourselves with some lonely holidays at times.

I know. I have been there.

Family relationships gone wrong leave us with an "arthritic" type of hurt, a bone-deep ache that can show up at different times in different places. It's part of the fellowship of Jesus' sufferings, beloved. Jesus came to

His own "and his own received him not" (John 1:11, KJV). During His earthly ministry, Jesus' brothers did not believe in Him and tried to tell Him how He should be making Himself known.[3] At one point they even decided He had taken leave of His senses.[4]

But Jesus didn't place earthly relationships above His relationship with the Father — and neither should we. Once when Jesus' family, including His mother, showed up and wanted to see Him, Jesus said to the person who brought the message, " 'Who is My mother and who are My brothers?' And stretching out His hand toward His disciples, He said, 'Behold My mother and My brothers! For whoever does the will of My Father who is in heaven, he is My brother and sister and mother' " (Matthew 12:48–50).

Our first responsibility is to the One who gave His all for us, and in Peter's first letter, we can glean some principles that I believe will help prepare us for the days that lie ahead.

Rejoice in Bringing Glory to God

In 1 Peter 1:6–7 we are assured that trials are necessary and prove our faith. When Jesus comes in all His glory, those very sufferings will bring praise, glory, and honor. Listen again to the Word of God:

> In this you greatly rejoice, even though now for a little while, if necessary, you have been distressed by various trials, so that the proof of your faith, being more precious than gold which is perishable, even though tested by fire, may be found to result in praise and glory and honor at the revelation of Jesus Christ.

So what are we to do? Rejoice!

When you rejoice, it takes the stinger out of suffering! It's your affirmation of faith in His sovereignty and sufficient grace.

We Have an Example to Follow

> For you have been called for this purpose, since Christ also suffered for you, leaving you an example for you to follow in His steps, who committed no sin, nor was any deceit found in His mouth; and while being reviled, He did not revile in return; while suffering, He uttered no threats, but kept entrusting Himself to Him who judges righteously. (1 Peter 2:21–23)

Do you see that word *example?* It's translated from an interesting Greek term that appears in only one other place in the New Testament. Literally it means "underwriting," which refers to a writing or drawing that a student reproduces.[5]

Can you see it?

A master artist sketches a scene, and then a student comes behind him and seeks to reproduce what the artist has just completed. In this case, Jesus is asking us to endure suffering in the way that He endured suffering. Let's take a quick look at a few of these "underwritings," or student sketches in 1 Peter 2:21–23.

Sketch #1: When Jesus suffered, He did not sin nor did He try to lie His way out of the situation. When you read the four Gospel accounts of His betrayal in the Garden of Gethsemane, His time at the house of Caiaphas, and what happened when He stood before Pilate, Herod, and then Pilate again, observe His words. Watch His response when the Roman soldiers mocked and scourged Him and when He was taunted as He hung on the cross. If you do, you'll become keenly aware that Jesus didn't react to what others did to Him. His flesh didn't rule. He remained in control of His response, refusing to be drawn into sin.

Sketch #2: When Jesus suffered, He controlled His mouth. So many times in the midst of hurt and pain we want to retaliate, to "let 'em have it," or "lay 'em low," don't we? I know I do. I may not be able to fight with my fists, but I have a mighty powerful tongue! How about you? It may be a little member of our bodies, but it carries the power of life and death.[6] But Jesus restrained Himself from lashing out with His tongue, even in the face of gross injustice. He didn't revile, bluster, threaten, or curse. And He even had time to speak a word of encouragement to needy ones on the way to His crucifixion.

Sketch #3: When Jesus suffered, He kept entrusting Himself to God, knowing that God judges righteously. Jesus kept His focus and didn't lose it. To "entrust" means to hand yourself over to another. As dark as His circumstances were in that hour, Jesus knew the Father was in control and counted on that. God had given Him this cup to drink. There was a purpose in His pain. (Oh, what a purpose!).

You and I are to do the same. In every affliction we are to remember, beloved, that God is in control. But not *only* in control. He will justly judge those who perpetrate our suffering. The truth will be known, and the afflicter dealt with. As Paul writes to the

Thessalonians:

> For after all it is only just for God to repay with affliction those who afflict you, and to give relief to you who are afflicted and to us as well when the Lord Jesus will be revealed from heaven with His mighty angels in flaming fire, dealing out retribution to those who do not know God and to those who do not obey the gospel of our Lord Jesus.
>
> These will pay the penalty of eternal destruction, away from the presence of the Lord and from the glory of His power, when He comes to be glorified in His saints on that day. (2 Thessalonians 1:6–10)

Trust that God *will* make it all right in the end. And all will know that we were not fools for trusting Him and placing ourselves into His hands!

Be Sure You're Suffering for the Right Reasons

Make sure your suffering is because of righteousness, not sin, and that you handle it in a godly way. Listen to 1 Peter 3:14–17:

> Even if you should suffer for the sake of

righteousness, you are blessed. And do not fear their intimidation, and do not be troubled, but sanctify Christ as Lord in your hearts, always being ready to make a defense to everyone who asks you to give an account for the hope that is in you, yet with gentleness and reverence; and keep a good conscience so that in the thing in which you are slandered, those who revile your good behavior in Christ will be put to shame. For it is better, if God should will it so, that you suffer for doing what is right rather than for doing what is wrong.

Prepare for Battle!

You are to prayerfully arm yourself, putting on your armor as carefully as a soldier prepares for battle.[7] You are to stand strong in whatever suffering God calls on you to endure — strong against the lure of sin, and strong against the lusts of the flesh. As Jesus suffered in the flesh, you must do the same. Make up your mind and settle it in your heart to do the will of God, whatever the cost. First Peter 4:1–2 says,

Therefore, since Christ has suffered in the flesh, arm yourselves also with the same purpose, because he who has suffered in the flesh has ceased from sin, so as to live the rest of the time in the flesh no longer for the lusts of men, but for the will of God.

Someone who arms himself or herself in this way has taken a determined stand against sin. Sin is not an option, because you are set on doing His will, no matter the cost.

Hold Tight to the Truth

Suffering is humbling; there's no doubt about that. But even so, we are not to run away from it. How then do you get through this painful process? You get through . . .

- by remembering God will eventually exalt you.
- by rolling every situation onto God's shoulders, knowing that what concerns you is of the utmost concern to Him and that He will never leave you or forsake you. He is your help.[8]
- by staying on the alert. The devil remains the devil, and he is out to devour you. Don't give in — resist.
- by remembering you are not alone in your suffering. Others are going through the same experiences.

- by remembering that your suffering had a beginning, and it will have an end. It is for a little while, in the light of your eternal glory.

Listen to your God through His servant, Peter, as he closed out his letter and I bring this chapter to a close.

> Therefore humble yourselves under the mighty hand of God, that He may exalt you at the proper time, casting all your anxiety on Him, because He cares for you. . . .
> After you have suffered for a little while, the God of all grace, who called you to His eternal glory in Christ, will Himself perfect, confirm, strengthen and establish you. (1 Peter 5:6–10)

If you will take these truths to heart, you'll be ready to handle any hurt that comes your way.

I pray you know you are loved.

CHAPTER SEVENTEEN:
HOW CAN JESUS POSSIBLY
UNDERSTAND YOUR PAIN?

Many of us go through life with a tidied-up, idealized, airbrushed image of the Lord Jesus. Maybe we grew up in Sunday school, seeing pictures of Him with a snowy white tunic, blue eyes, wavy brown hair, and neatly trimmed beard. Or perhaps we found ourselves admiring depictions of Him in a stained glass window in some church sanctuary, with refracted sunlight pouring through an unearthly face, surrounded by a golden halo.

We can't imagine such a man getting His hands dirty, raising His voice, experiencing emotions — in short, being *human.* As a result, when we find ourselves bruised and bleeding from the blows of life or staggering under a load of deep anxiety or emotional pain, we don't instinctively think of turning to Jesus for help.

After all, we might reason, He is holy. He is separate. He is seated on a throne in heaven, surrounded by mighty angels and saints from days of old. What does He know of the huge mess of my circumstances, heartache in my marriage or family, or the splintered, jagged shards of my broken dreams?

The New Testament, however, paints a very different picture.

Though He was and is God, Jesus turned His back on the magnificent glory of heaven to become a real, flesh-and-blood Man . . . a Man who knew physical pain, went toe to toe with Satan, faced up to innumerable temptations, was rejected by His own, tasted the bitterness of disappointment and sorrow, and experienced a full range of human emotions.

You can't understand Calvary's love — its hell or its healing — until you gain a true picture of what Jesus endured on our behalf. Your healing rests on what was done almost two thousand years ago when Jesus, who knew no sin, was made sin for you and me.

In the Garden of Gethsemane, shortly before His death, Jesus had to face the darkest hour of His earthly life to that point. This is where He had to come to terms with the will of His Father and submit to the inconceivable horror of taking upon Himself all the sins of the world, for all time.

The very thought of it nearly crushed the life from His body.

Then Jesus came with them to a place called Gethsemane, and said to His disciples, "Sit here while I go over there and pray." And He took with Him Peter and the two sons of Zebedee, and began to be grieved and distressed. Then He said to them, "My soul is deeply grieved, to the point of death; remain here and keep watch with Me."

And He went a little beyond them, and fell on His face and prayed, saying, "My Father, if it is possible, let this cup pass from Me; yet not as I will, but as You will." (Matthew 26:36–39)

Another New Testament picture, not so well known, gives us a different view of those same terrible minutes in the night shadows of that hillside olive garden. As I explained in a previous chapter, the book of Hebrews was written to suffering, persecuted believers who were, in some cases, so discouraged that they felt like throwing in the towel and going back to their Jewish faith. To better touch their downcast hearts, the writer gave them a glimpse of what Jesus went through to bring them salvation and forgiveness of sins. Listen to these graphic words:

> In the days of His flesh, He offered up both prayers and supplications with loud crying and tears to the One able to save Him from death, and He was heard because of His piety. Although He was a Son, He learned obedience from the things which He suffered. And having been made perfect, He became to all those who obey Him the source of eternal salvation. (Hebrews 5:7–9)

Prayers. Supplications. Loud crying. Tears.
This is no made-up Jesus who is more a religious symbol than a genuine human being. This is a living, breathing, authentic Man who, in the weakness of flesh, did not want to drink "the cup."

So He prayed. He agonized. With a heart that felt like lead in His chest, He cried — hard — with loud sobs and real tears flowing down His face. In that garden, He went to the Father three separate times, asking if there was any other way to redeem man, if there was any possible way He could bypass the cross and still achieve the purpose for which He had come.

But there was no other way, so He willingly walked that road to Calvary.

Does He understand your secret sorrows, your bone-deep disappointments, and your sometimes crushing anxieties?

Yes! Yes, He does.

Have you ever been betrayed by someone close to you?

A business associate? A family member? A trusted friend? Your own husband or wife? Your child?

Of all the hurts in life, those perpetrated by someone we love and trust may go deepest.

If you allow the memory to remain in your thoughts, it will prey upon your mind, shred any hope of peace, and create the environment for toxic bitterness.

David once wrote:

All who hate me whisper together against
  me;
  Against me they devise my hurt. . . .
Even my close friend in whom I trusted,
  Who ate my bread,
    Has lifted up his heel against me.
    (Psalm 41:7–9)

It must have been hard for David to get that betrayal out of his mind. And let's be honest, it's hard for you and me too, isn't it? How could that individual do that to you after all you had meant to each other? And did they do it deceptively, "with a kiss"? It just wasn't right . . .

Jesus understands.

Jesus knew Judas would betray Him, and yet for about three and a half years they were virtually inseparable. Judas was one of the Twelve, chosen after a night in prayer. Yet Judas was "a devil."[1]

On more than one occasion, Jesus told the disciples He would be betrayed into the hands of His enemies and then crucified. The disciples, however, just didn't seem to get it. Was that stark fact somehow hidden from their understanding . . . or were they simply in denial?

On the very night in which Judas would betray Him, Jesus washed the traitor's feet in the upper room before sharing the Passover meal with the Twelve.

And then, all too quickly, His hour came.

The powers of darkness closed in.

We can't even imagine what a heavy heart Jesus had in those moments as they left the city, walked past the temple, headed down into the Kidron Valley, and then up to the Garden of Gethsemane.

"Gethsemane" means olive press. And no

man was ever pressed like Jesus was on that night of agony.

Have you ever cried to God, asking Him to rescue you, to let you escape, to save you from the horror you were about to experience — and He didn't?

Jesus understands.

He lived in a body of flesh, knowing full well its weaknesses and vulnerabilities. When Jesus arrived in Gethsemane, He went a stone's throw away from His disciples, and there, alone, He pleaded with "Abba, Father" to take the cup from Him. Wasn't there another way — a way of less pain and separation? He knew that with God all things were possible. Three times Jesus asked, "Father, if You are willing, remove this cup from Me; yet not My will, but Yours be done" (Luke 22:42).

Only God could have brought a halt to the events about to be set in motion, events that would bring such excruciating agony, humiliation, and pain to His Son.

But He didn't.

Why? Because He had a higher purpose in mind.

Have you ever been abandoned or disowned by someone who had vowed to never leave you, to stay with you no matter what happened?

Jesus understands.

As he was leaving the upper room with Jesus and the others, Peter confidently asserted that even if everyone else fell away and left Jesus, *he* never would. "Even if I have to die with You," he told the Lord, "I will not deny You" (Mark 14:31).

Jesus wasn't in the garden long before Judas came. A Roman cohort and officers from the chief priests and Pharisees accompanied Judas, lighting the dark with their lanterns and torches, weapons clanging against their armor. Judas betrayed his Master with a kiss, and they proceeded to bind and arrest Jesus.

Valiantly Peter drew his sword and with one wild swing cut off the ear of the high priest's slave. But once they arrested Jesus, Peter followed at a distance. When they arrived at the house of Caiaphas, Peter was quickly identified as being a follower of Jesus, but he denied it — not once, but three times.

Have you ever been abused, beaten, spit on, falsely accused, or called a liar?

Jesus understands.

When He was taken to the house of Caiaphas, the high priest, He was falsely accused and lied about by men who were determined to bring about His death. His life meant nothing to them. Jesus was in their way, and they wanted to destroy Him. When He, the Truth, spoke the truth, they called it blasphemy. Then they watched as others made sport of Jesus. Blindfolding Him, they spit at Him, beat Him with their fists, slapped Him, and mocked Him.

Isaiah the prophet foretold of this time. "I gave My back to those who strike Me, and My cheeks to those who pluck out the beard; I did not cover My face from humiliation and spitting" (50:6).

Have you ever been abused and then locked in a closet, a basement, or put into some sort of a pit? Left shivering in the cold darkness of a place without light?

Jesus understands.

Under Roman law, the Jews were allowed to give their criminals thirty-nine lashes with a whip. To this day, if you visit Jerusalem, you can see where Jesus was incarcerated in the house of Caiaphas. You can see where they tied the arms and legs of their prisoners and then proceeded to whip them. You can also see a hollowed-out bowl where the sponge with vinegar was held. Vinegar?

Yes, to pour on the raw, seething wounds in order to produce maximum agony. You can go down into the pit, the dry cistern where, bruised and beaten, Jesus was lowered by ropes to spend the night alone in the damp darkness.

Have you ever been paraded before others who could have helped you and come to your defense, but they didn't? Have you ever been forced to stand all alone?

Jesus understands.

He was taken from the house of Caiaphas and delivered to Pilate — His face undoubtedly black and blue, grotesquely swollen from the blows He had received the night before. His beard would have been patchy with dried blood, from where they pulled out the hair.[2] His back would certainly have been bloody, bruised, and cut from the whipping.

Think of it! Here was God in the flesh, bound with shackles and standing before an earthly governor.

Know this, beloved: He stood there all alone. No one stood with Him. No one came to His defense. No one sought to rescue Him.

Have you ever been looked on as an object

of curiosity? You meant nothing more than a source of amusement to those looking on. Or maybe you were asked to entertain someone who was used to getting anything and everything he wanted? Have you ever been forced to dress in a way you found demeaning, even humiliating?

Jesus understands.

From Pilate, Jesus was taken to Herod. What was the reasoning there? Just this: if Jesus claimed to be king of the Jews, then why not send Him to the one who claimed that title for himself? It was a pass-off of responsibility; Pilate and Herod were anything but friends until after that day. Herod, however, was eager to see Jesus — even hoping he might see Jesus perform some sort of a sign. Although Herod plied Him with questions, Jesus didn't respond to the evil king. As a result, Herod showed his contempt and disdain for Jesus by dressing Him in one of his own royal robes as a form of mockery and then sending Him back to Pilate.

Have you ever had people make sport of you or use you as an object of scorn? Have you been delivered over to the will of evil people? Been beaten until you were unrecognizable?

Jesus understands.

He was sent to the Praetorium and handed to the soldiers — restless, brutal men who were mostly confined to their barracks. They were stationed in Jerusalem to suppress any possible uprising during the Passover festival.

Now the Praetorian guard held Jesus in their power, this so-called King and Savior. They took off the robe Herod had put on Jesus' shoulders and began their scourging with the infamous cat-o'-nine-tails. This whip consisted of nine leather straps, each bearing metal hooks. In the hands of an accomplished scourger, the whip could pull ribbons of flesh neatly off the back and stomach, leaving them hanging like a fringe and exposing the bowels of the victim. The object was to bring the prisoner close to death without killing him outright.

The mockery continued, as one of the soldiers had the idea to weave a crown out of the thorn branches used for firewood and to put on Jesus the purple robe reserved for kings. Can you imagine the mocking laughter echoing through that cavernous Roman barracks? The prisoner had claimed He was a king — and kings must have crowns!

Finally the games were over. It was time to take Jesus to Golgotha, "the place of the skull." When they pulled off the purple robe, stuck like glue to His bleeding back, the pain must have been excruciating. Dressing Him once again in His own seamless tunic, they laid the cross on His back and made Him march. But He didn't get far, and when He stumbled, they pulled a man off the street, Simon from Cyrene, to bear the cross to Calvary.

Have you ever endured excruciating pain — pain so agonizing that you nearly begged for the relief of death? Have you ever had spikes driven through your hands and feet . . . or been strung up nude . . . or thought you were going to suffocate . . . or been shamed beyond belief?

Jesus understands.

They stripped Him naked, laid His seeping body in the dirt, and nailed his hands to the crossbar. The nail hit the nerve running through the wrist, and the fingers on His hands curled with pain. Then they lifted His dangling body and dropped the crossbar into the notch of an upright, outside the Damascus gate on the well-traveled road connecting Jerusalem to Damascus.

Every breath brought agony, and that breath would only come as He pushed His raw back up against the bark of the felled tree that held Him. His words were short. He could only tolerate the pain in His feet for a short time as He strained against the nails. He was poured out like water.

And He knew, "Cursed is everyone who hangs on a tree" (Galatians 3:13).

Have you ever been mocked? Accused? Verbally abused? Stared at because you were so distorted as a human being? Have you listened to the taunts of those who declared you to be a fraud, who said that if there were a God and you were of any value, He would have rescued you?

Jesus understands.

They stared at Him. Isaiah tells us, "His appearance was marred more than any man and His form more than the sons of men" (52:14). In other words, Jesus was barely recognizable as a human being.

In the midst of such agony, spectators and passersby railed at Him. Sneered. Hurled abuse. Wagged their heads. Challenged His relationship to God. If He was the Son of God, why didn't He come off the cross? If He trusted in God, why didn't God rescue Him?

Another man hanging on his own cross near Jesus insulted Him and blasphemed.

Jesus despised the shame but endured the

cross for the joy that was set before Him.[3] That joy is your redemption.

Have you ever taken someone else's penalty? Gotten the punishment they deserved, while they escaped unscathed?

Jesus understands.

Jesus was not born in sin. He was not a sinner. He was tempted by the same serpent of old who tempted Adam and Eve, but He didn't yield. He resisted the devil, always and only doing what pleased the Father. Yet the One who knew no sin was made to be sin for us.[4] Jesus took the wages of sin on Himself. When He hung on the cross in utter agony, God placed the sins of all mankind for all of time on Jesus. He did this to free us from sin and from the payment for sin, which is eternal death in the lake of fire. In so doing, He rendered Satan powerless when it comes to death.

As you remember, in the Garden of Gethsemane Jesus asked the Father if there was another way — if the cup could pass from Him.

But there was no other way, and He drank that cup to its dregs.

And what was Jesus saying as He hung on the cross? "Jesus was saying, 'Father, forgive them; for they do not know what they are doing' " (Luke 23:34).

Have you ever felt yourself forsaken by God? You cried, but He didn't come through; He didn't rescue you from the moment?

Jesus understands.

He was forsaken. Forsaken by His Father. Forsaken by the Spirit.

Darkness fell at noon — the sixth hour. About the ninth hour, three in the afternoon, "Jesus cried out with a loud voice saying, 'Eli, Eli, lama sabachthani?,' that is, 'My God, My God, why have You forsaken Me?' " (Matthew 27:46). The sins of mankind had been placed upon His shoulders.

Right after that, Jesus cried out again with a loud voice: "Tetelestai!" Translation? *"It is finished"* (John 19:30).

The debt of all the sins of all time was paid in full, once for all.[5] Jesus was forsaken so you could be forgiven and never ever be forsaken.

Although He [Jesus] was a Son, He learned obedience from the things which He suffered. And having been made perfect, He became to all those who obey Him the source of eternal salvation. . . . (Hebrews 5:8–9)

324

Jesus understands your suffering, your pain . . . the hurt that runs deep.

Have you ever truly thanked Him for what He suffered for you? If not, why don't you open your Bible and read Psalm 22 and thank Him for so great a love.

Do it now, beloved of God. Let all that He suffered on your behalf be a healing salve to your heart.

And remember this:

When the hurt runs deep, God's love is deeper still.

CHAPTER EIGHTEEN:
WILL THE HURT EVER GO AWAY?

It was their stepmother's ninety-first birthday, and all of Nancy's brothers and sisters would be there. When Nancy prayed about what they were to do, God clearly laid it on her heart that she was to wash the family's feet.

Even as she questioned Him, God still impressed on her heart, *"Wash your father's and stepmother's feet. Also, wash the feet of your brothers and sisters. When you do, the old will be gone, and you will have a brand-new unity among the entire family."*

But . . . how could she do such a thing?

This was the father who had abandoned his wife after beating her with a boot. Nancy's mother had been twenty-five at the time and pregnant with her sixth child after eight years of marriage. Nancy had watched the beating, crying and screaming until her dad told her that if she didn't shut up, she would get some of the same.

Hiding behind the refrigerator, this three-and-a-half-year-old girl watched her father gather up his two older sons and walk out while his wife lay bleeding on the floor. He left behind three little girls — Nancy and a younger and older sister. Her mother later gave birth to a little boy.

A few years later, Nancy's older sister left to find their father, and Nancy became the little mother to her brother and sister. Her own mother, an alcoholic, was unable to care for the children.

Nancy was nine when her mother took the children to a Memorial Day rodeo in a small nearby town. During this supposed "family outing," Nancy's mother handed her over to total strangers, who put her in the backseat of their car with a bunch of kids. Her mother was giving away her daughter! As the car door slammed shut, Nancy looked out the open window to see her sister and brother standing in the back of a stranger's pickup truck, crying and begging her to come back.

Nancy threw such a fit that the people let her out of the car, and she went to collect her siblings. She never learned who the people were that her mother had left them with.

That night the young threesome walked

home all by themselves. Their mother had simply abandoned them. Although relatives lived in their small town, none came to care for them. And even though their mother's brother was a police officer in the town, Jackie, Jimmie, and Nancy lived alone for several months.

No one cared. After all, these kids didn't amount to much. They were Mary Lou's kids, and everybody knew Mary Lou was a "no-good alcoholic."

Nancy cooked potatoes over a candle, or she'd take Jackie and Jimmie to the diner, order water, and put ketchup and salt and pepper in it. Nancy washed their clothes in the bathtub and did her best to take care of them. They would walk the town holding hands, looking for their mother. At night Nancy would scoot her bed to the window and try to stay awake . . . convinced that, if only she could keep her eyes open, her mother would come back.

But she didn't.

It would be years before they saw their mother again.

BITTERNESS TAKES ROOT

Several months passed, and then Child Welfare showed up. Bundled into a car, the children were taken to a town about forty miles away. Once again Nancy threw a tantrum. She was convinced her mother was coming back — and wouldn't find them. The tantrum didn't work. Her father met the ladies from Welfare and put Jackie and Nancy in his truck, but he refused to take Jimmy despite the pleas of the two girls. He didn't think Jimmy was his son.

It was at this time that a root of bitterness dropped into the furrowed soil of Nancy's young heart. Living with their father and stepmother took them into an atmosphere of religious rules and rigid structure — without any expression of love. Their dad was a bitter man who fell into rages of verbal and physical abuse.

When Nancy turned ten, she received her first Bible and learned that there was a God who would listen to prayer. So every night Jackie and Nancy scooted their beds together, crossed their legs, held hands, and pleaded with God to give them back their brother Jimmy.

Month after month they prayed, yet nothing happened. Convinced that prayer didn't work, Nancy refused to pray any more. Although her little sister begged and cried, Nancy held her ground. She was not going to pray! When Jackie refused to stop crying, however, Nancy finally acquiesced. It was a

Friday night.

Saturday was the day Dad came home after working a week in another town. It was just after lunch. Two people got out of the truck — and one of them was Jimmy. It was Nancy's first answer to prayer. Two little girls had been heard by the Sovereign Ruler of the universe.

After church one Sunday, the family drove to a big house filled with kids. Lots of adults came to the house also and watched as the children paraded around a huge living room. It wasn't until later that Nancy realized why they weren't allowed to go outside and play with the other children, and why they had to keep their church clothes nice. Her father was trying to get them adopted! But nobody wanted them.

When Nancy was sixteen, her father put her in his pickup truck and dropped her and her clothes in front of a house in the same town they had lived in when Nancy was nine. Her mother had returned — but she didn't know Nancy was coming home.

Alcohol was still Mary Lou's closest friend. Living with her was hell, and Nancy could only bear it until her junior year of high school. After that, she moved to a boarding house, paying her rent from part-time jobs until she graduated.

Mary Lou died of cirrhosis of the liver when Nancy was nineteen. By this time, she was an angry, bitter young woman filled with rage and armed with a defense mechanism that could win wars.

When Nancy married in her twenties, her only vice was alcohol. She and her husband both drank, but they could handle it — or so they thought. Ten years and two children later they decided to call it quits on their marriage. Even the minister at church advised it, "because you've already divorced him in your heart." But the minister had never so much as opened a Bible in any of their counseling sessions.

As a single mom supporting two children, Nancy had little time to be the mother she wanted to be, so once again she turned to the God who had brought Jimmy back. This time she requested a husband. God answered, and Mike loved the children. They moved to Virginia to leave Nancy's past behind.

TURMOIL WITHIN

Nancy was in a new place, but she couldn't shake the turmoil within. She would later describe "the depression, the guilt, the shame, the defensiveness, the anger, rage, bitterness, and the fear of abandonment." It all moved to Virginia with her.

But something else happened in Virginia as well. Something wonderful.

Nancy heard about the love of God and the death of Jesus on the cross — and that her sins could be forgiven. "Forgiveness for my sins," she recalled, "meant a lot to me, when I thought about the many bars, taverns, and numerous other forsaken places I had frequented."[1] It was at the cross of Christ that Nancy found what she'd been looking for all those years.

Nancy became a living witness to the freedom that comes when the Son sets you free. She was free indeed! Forgiven, freed from the power of sin, headed to heaven, and convinced God would never abandon her or forsake her.

But the hurt still ran deep.

"The hurt was real, and the pain had cut a deep ravine through my heart. A nontrusting, anxious ravine that I thought I could not heal even as a Christian . . . until I found the book *Lord, Heal My Hurts*."[2]

Not only did Nancy study the book — a study God had led me to write for hurting people like her! — she began teaching it to others. It was the water of God's Word, along with prayer, that brought her to the place where she was willing to wash the feet of the father she had forgiven.[3]

When Nancy washed her parents' feet, placing them in the same basin, "I told them how much I loved them, and how grateful I was for the time they had spent in my life. I told them I had gleaned good things from the time I had been with them and how I wanted to be a servant of God. By washing their feet, I wanted to honor them as the parents God had given me."[4]

Because Nancy understood what happened at the cross, she was able to say those words as she washed her father's feet in the basin of water and dried them with a towel.

Her father looked up at her, tears running down his face, and said, "I can finally go. I can finally go now."

It really doesn't matter whether your hurts have been caused by someone else's actions, or by your own sins and failures. The solution, beloved, remains the same.

Healing and forgiveness begin at the cross.

New life rests in your understanding of what Jesus accomplished on the cross, and your day-by-day, hour-by-hour choice to bring your thoughts, emotions, and behavior in line with that living reality.

The cross is essentially about four things: love, sin, forgiveness of sin, and redemption from sin. It is sin — yours, someone else's, society's — that is the root cause of hurt, pain, suffering, and death. The cure is in understanding and embracing the love of God, which "undid" sin and broke its power.

WHERE HEALING BEGINS

In so many of the e-mails I've received through the years and in the conversations I've shared with those who have experienced deep hurt, I am asked the same questions: "Will the hurt never go away? Will it damage me for the rest of my life?"

From what I have learned in my own personal inductive study of the Word of God, I believe that *you will experience healing to the degree that you believe and apply His Word to your life.* I believe healing is a matter of faith — moment by moment, incident by incident, day by day. God had Jeremiah write, "Heal me, O LORD, and I will be healed" (17:14). And I believe that.

HEALING TRUTH #12

Whether your hurts have been caused by someone else's actions or by your own sins and failures, healing begins at the cross — the greatest expression of God's love for you.

Where does healing begin? For me it begins at the cross — the greatest expression God the Father, God the Son, and God the Spirit could give of their love to you. In the previous chapter I gave you just a smattering of what happened in the death of Jesus Christ. It was a death that was necessary because of sin, and a death that brought complete forgiveness of sin. What's more, Christ's death for us secured our redemption from sin's penalty, sin's power, and eventually, from sin's very presence . . . forever!

Volumes have been written on this subject, and volumes more could be added to that mountain of material. But one book covers it all: it's the Book written by God Himself. The more you discipline yourself to diligently study the Bible rather than rely on the writings of men, the more deeply you will experience His healing. A divine interaction takes place when you feed on the Word of God and, in the process, store it in your heart and your mind so you can meditate on it.[5]

There is no other book in all the world like the Bible, where the words have been breathed by God Himself and are supernaturally infused with life.

Then they cried out to the LORD in their
  trouble;
He saved them out of their distresses.
He sent His word and healed them,
  and delivered them from their destruc-
  tions. (Psalm 107:19–20)

Complete healing will never come if you
don't first believe that all your sins are
forgiven — forgiven by God Almighty, by
His Son, and by His Spirit. Until you accept this fact by faith, there will always be a
shadow between you and God, a shadow
where lies and unjust condemnation lurk in
the darkness of unbelief.

Healing begins with believing God when
He says, "Your sins have been forgiven"
(Luke 7:48). When Jesus died on the cross,
He "offered one sacrifice for sins for all
time" (Hebrews 10:12). In light of this God
says, " 'And their sins and their lawless
deeds I will remember no more.' Now where
there is forgiveness of these things, there is
no longer any offering for sin" (Hebrews
10:17–18).

There is absolutely nothing you can do to
pay for your sin. Jesus did it for you. Believe
it.

Are you responding, "Okay, okay, but
what if I can't forgive *myself*?" Oh dear one,

that is messed-up thinking! It was God's laws you broke. If God has forgiven you, you are forgiven. You either believe it or you don't. If you don't, you are sinning against God. What more does He have to do? The answer is "nothing," because He has done it all.

Cast aside those thoughts of self-condemnation, and fill your vision with Jesus, the One who loves you and died for you. Get on your face, beloved of God, and don't get up until you repent — change your mind — and believe that Jesus has paid it all.

EXTENDING FORGIVENESS TO OTHERS

Now, once you know and understand that you are forgiven of your sins, you need to forgive others.

"But why should I forgive?" you may say. "Why let them off the hook? They need to pay! If I forgive them, then they'll go free."

You're right, they shouldn't go free after what they did. So let's see what God says. Let's begin with what is called the Lord's Prayer.

Have you ever prayed the Lord's Prayer, the example Jesus offered when the disciples asked Him to teach them to pray? These words are familiar to many, but when did you last consider them closely? Please read the words carefully. In fact, why don't you read them aloud?

"Pray, then, in this way:
'Our Father who is in heaven,
Hallowed be Your name.
Your kingdom come.
Your will be done,
On earth as it is in heaven.
Give us this day our daily bread.
And forgive us our debts, as we also have forgiven our debtors.
And do not lead us into temptation, but deliver us from evil.
For Yours is the kingdom and the power and the glory forever. Amen.' " (Matthew 6:9–13)

Did you hear the words *forgive* and *forgiven?* Got your pencil? Why don't you read it again and underline them.

Did you notice the word *as?* Circle it. According to Jesus, we are to ask God to forgive us our debts *as* we have forgiven our debtors. In other words, forgiveness is not optional if we want to be in relationship with God; it is a required act of obedience.

Listen to what He says in Matthew 6:14–15:

"For if you forgive others for their transgressions, your heavenly Father will also forgive you. But if you do not forgive others, then your Father will not forgive your transgressions."

Did you notice the words *for* and *but*?

Think with me for a moment; let's reason truth together. Through the death of Jesus Christ, God has guaranteed forgiveness of all our sins. The penalty for sin, which is death, has been paid in full. Sin's power has been broken. You have moved from the kingdom and the dominion of Satan to the kingdom of God. Because your sins have been paid for in full, Satan no longer has the power of death over you.[6] Having believed, you are now sealed with the Holy Spirit of promise. The Spirit *in you* is your ticket, so to speak, to heaven. He is the guarantee of your redemption from the presence of sin and your entrance into God's eternal kingdom.[7]

However, even though you are no longer a slave to sin, you can still *choose* to sin. When you do, you have an advocate with the Father — a lawyer who paid the penalty for that sin and who now pleads your case. His name is Jesus Christ. So what do you do? You confess that sin, name it for what it is, and ask for forgiveness. And because you want to be right with God and do what is right, God forgives just as you asked.

But don't forget this: according to what you saw in the Lord's Prayer, you also are asking for forgiveness *on the basis of your forgiving your debtors* — those who owe you, as you owed God!

THE CONSEQUENCE OF UNFORGIVENESS

If, however, you are not willing to forgive, then according to Jesus, God withholds the forgiveness you have asked for, because you are sinning in not forgiving!

Perhaps you're thinking, *But that's not fair! That's not right!*

Not fair? Who are you to pass judgment on Creator God? You'd better pause and think about that. For a child of God to not forgive another human being is to sin. Do you remember looking earlier at Ephesians 4? Let me write out Ephesians 4:31–32 again, and include Ephesians 5:1–2 as well, because they flow together.

Let all bitterness and wrath and anger and clamor and slander be put away from you, along with all malice. Be kind to one another, tender-hearted, forgiving each other, just as God in Christ also has forgiven you.

Therefore be imitators of God, as beloved children; and walk in love, just as Christ also loved you and gave Himself up for us, an offering and a sacrifice to God as a fragrant aroma.

Did you notice what is to be put away? It's what Nancy had to put away as she forgave her father: *bitterness*. Bitterness left to itself breeds wrath and anger — which explodes into clamor! What is clamor? It's raising your voice, yelling and screaming. And where does clamor lead? It leads to *slander* — vicious words intended to cut down and destroy.

It all hurts, doesn't it? It carves the ravine of pain even deeper. It hurts others, but it also hurts you. Such behavior hurts you physically and emotionally, mentally and spiritually.

And how do you stop it? By forgiving.

But how do you forgive?

By focusing on the cross. By remembering what Jesus endured so you could be forgiven by God. By remembering what Jesus said as He hung on that cross, "Father, forgive them; for they do not know what they are doing" (Luke 23:34).

To forgive is to walk in love and give yourself up — to become a living sacrifice for the love of God just as Jesus did. Oh, what a sweet fragrance you become to your Creator and Redeemer! When we forgive, we demonstrate our redemption from sin.

And more than that: Forgiveness brings *healing.* Forgiveness loosens the hold the past has on our lives.

To refuse to forgive, by contrast, locks us in an emotional prison where *we* bear the punishment, *not* the perpetrator. And here's the strange aspect to all of this: the key to our prison cell is on our side of the door! We can be set free whenever we choose.

Of all the Scriptures on the subject of forgiveness, after the teaching on the cross, Jesus' words in Matthew 18 are the clearest. You need to read His teaching for yourself before we talk about it:

> Then Peter came and said to Him, "Lord, how often shall my brother sin against me and I forgive him? Up to seven times?" (v. 21)

Rabbinical law said three times; Peter thought he was being magnanimous.

Jesus said to him, "I do not say to you,

up to seven times, but up to seventy times seven." (v. 22)

Likely Peter was taken aback. So Jesus used a story to explain clearly what God's kingdom is all about in respect to forgiving

"For this reason the kingdom of heaven may be compared to a king who wished to settle accounts with his slaves. When he had begun to settle them, one who owed him ten thousand talents was brought to him. But since he did not have the means to repay, his lord commanded him to be sold, along with his wife and children and all that he had, and repayment to be made. So the slave fell to the ground and prostrated himself before him, saying, 'Have patience with me and I will repay you everything.' And the lord of that slave felt compassion and released him and forgave him the debt." (vv. 23–27)

Did you notice the words *compassion, released, forgave*?

"But that slave went out and found one of his fellow slaves who owed him a hundred denarii; and he seized him and began to choke him, saying, 'Pay back what you owe.' So his fellow slave fell to the ground and began to plead with him, saying, 'Have patience with me and I will repay you.' But he was unwilling and went and threw him in prison until he should pay back what was owed. So when his fellow slaves saw what had happened, they were deeply grieved and came and reported to their lord all that had happened." (vv. 28–31)

Stop and think about why these fellow slaves were deeply grieved. What is incongruous? What doesn't seem just about this man's behavior?

"Then summoning him, his lord said to him, 'You wicked slave, I forgave you all that debt because you pleaded with me. Should you not also have had mercy on your fellow slave, in the same way that I had mercy on you?' And his lord, moved with anger, handed him over to the torturers until he should repay all that was owed him." (vv. 32–34)

The story has ended. So what is the conclusion? What point did Jesus want His followers to get? Look at the next verse.

"My heavenly Father will also do the

same to you, if each of you does not forgive his brother from your heart." (v. 35)

Can you see the gravity of refusing to forgive *as* He has forgiven us? It means torture for you. Is that what you want? To be turned over to the torturers? What does that really mean, anyway? In the 40-Minute study *Forgiveness: Breaking the Power of the Past*, it's explained this way:

Torturers, a noun derived from the Greek verb *basaniz,* is used elsewhere to refer to sicknesses (Matthew 4:24; 8:6) and adverse circumstances (Matthew 14:24). God uses these things to correct wrong attitudes and produce proper spirits in His children (1 Corinthians 11:30–32). These torturers may be seen in our lives as difficult circumstances, sickness, bitterness, jealousy, anger, etc. Remember, Jesus is addressing Peter and the other disciples; His message is directed to believers, not unbelievers.[8]

What quality is a merciful God calling His forgiven people to demonstrate? Mercy.

In the beatitudes from the Sermon on the Mount, Jesus said, "Blessed are the merciful, for they shall receive mercy" (Matthew 5:7). James warns us, "For judgment will be merciless to one who has shown no mercy; mercy triumphs over judgment" (2:13).

In other words, judgment is *God's* business, not ours. Abraham once asked, "Shall not the Judge of all the earth deal justly?"[9] And we can answer with confidence, *Yes, He will.* God will most certainly deal with the one who caused you such pain and hurt and made you suffer.

Oh beloved, if you will live at the cross, God Himself will fill the ravine of your pain, where the hurt runs deep, with living waters, healing waters . . . "a river of the water of life, clear as crystal, coming from the throne of God and of the Lamb" (Revelation 22:1).

Conclusion: Life-Preserving Words

Persevere. Endure. Exult.

These are three good verbs from God's Word.

They are words that describe the path God desires for every one of His sons and daughters . . . even when the hurt runs deep.

According to the dictionary, to *persevere* means "to persist in anything undertaken . . . to maintain a purpose in spite of difficulty, obstacles, or discouragement . . . to continue steadfastly." As I often say to my Precept students as we study the Word of God, "Hangeth thou in there!"

James 1:12 gives us this encouragement to persevere: "Blessed is a man who perseveres under trial; for once he has been approved, he will receive the crown of life which the Lord has promised to those who love Him."

The second word, *endure*, means "to hold out against . . . to sustain without yielding . . . to bear with patience."

The whole New Testament book of Hebrews resounds with that anthem.

Therefore, do not throw away your confidence, which has a great reward. For you have need of endurance, so that when you have done the will of God, you may receive what was promised. . . . Therefore, since we have so great a cloud of witnesses surrounding us, let us also lay aside every encumbrance and the sin which so easily entangles us, and let us run with endurance the race that is set before us. (Hebrews 10:35–36, 12:1)

Persevere.
Endure.
Those are good, solid words — right out of the pages of Scripture — that describe the duty of every true child of God, no matter the trial, the test, or temptation. These are words that lift your head, square your shoulders, put steel into your spine, and give strength to your feet to stay on the path.
Persevere.
Endure.
The Old Testament provides rich examples of those who did, and the New Testament gives the command to follow in their foot-

steps. This is the stuff of genuine faith, the disciplines that keep us strong through all the tribulations of life.

In the book of Romans, God, through the apostle Paul, makes it clear that having been justified by faith, we have peace with God and stand permanently in the grace of God. As a result, we can be truly glad and joyful in the hope of coming glory. This is a sure hope secured by the death and resurrection of Jesus Christ.[1]

But while we have peace with God, we will not find peace with all men. Heaven is our hope of glory, but life here on earth will contain tribulation, just as Jesus told His disciples: "In the world you have tribulation, but take courage; I have overcome the world" (John 16:33).

We live in an unconverted world, a world governed by the prince of darkness, a ruler who is actively at work in the lives of those who have not placed their faith and trust in Jesus the Redeemer.

It is the sin of mankind that causes much of our hurt — hurt that can run deep unto death. Yet even in this we are to exult.

Exult. That's the third verb that tells us how to live.

What does it mean to exult? You'll like this, because *exult* is an immensely happy word. The dictionary defines it this way: "To show or feel a lively or triumphant joy . . . to rejoice exceedingly . . . to be highly elated or jubilant . . . to leap upward, especially for joy."

How long has it been since you literally jumped for joy?

Maybe it's time you got out your jumping shoes.

THE PATH TO HOPE AND JOY

Why should we rejoice in such a way when we live in a world with so much hurt, disappointment, and brokenness? Listen to the Word of God Almighty:

> Therefore, having been justified by faith, we have peace with God through our Lord Jesus Christ, through whom also we have obtained our introduction by faith into this grace in which we stand; and we exult [there's our word!] in hope of the glory of God. *And not only this, but we also exult in our tribulations,* knowing that tribulation brings about perseverance; and perseverance, proven character; and proven character, hope; and hope does not disappoint, because the love of God has been poured out within our hearts through the Holy Spirit who

was given to us. (Romans 5:1–5)

The tribulation we endure in all its varied forms and ways, and the hurts that ensue, brings perseverance and endurance.

And those are flat-out beautiful words.

It is perseverance that shapes us, puts us to the test, proves us, and finds us genuine, approved by God. And listen, beloved: that proven character, purified in the fire of tribulation, brings *hope.*

Why hope? Because we have seen and are assured that what we possess is completely authentic and can never be taken away from us. It is hope that does not disappoint, because our faith is real and a joyful eternity awaits us.

This is why we are to exult. To experience the wild happiness of heaven. To count it all joy, as James records in this command from God:

Consider it all joy, my brethren, when you encounter various trials, knowing that the testing of your faith produces endurance. And let endurance have its perfect result, so that you may be perfect and complete, lacking in nothing. (James 1:2–4)

The word translated *perseverance* in

Romans 5 and *endurance* in James 1 is the same Greek word, *hupomone,* and means "to abide under." In other words, "Don't quit. Don't surrender. Don't give up. Don't walk away."

In explaining some of the shades of meaning in the original language, one commentator speaks of *hupomone* as "the characteristic of a man who is not swerved from his deliberate purpose and his loyalty to faith and piety by even the greatest trials and sufferings."[2]

Perseverance and endurance speak of loyalty in our faith and testify to the fact that we believe in God and will not consider quitting, giving up, turning back, or walking away.

When James says, "Consider it all joy" when you encounter trials, the word *consider* means literally to lead, to command. This is what you are to do at all times, even when the hurt runs deep. You *lead* with joy — one of the ninefold attributes of the fruit of the Spirit — as you persevere and endure. You keep putting one foot in front of another in the race that is set before you. And you exult in knowing that you have a hope that does not, will not, disappoint!

THE DANGER OF NEGLECTING GOD'S WORD AND HIS PEOPLE

As I have said, the book of Hebrews urges believers to persevere and endure through every trial and heartache, and its message is for each and every one of us. It was originally written to first-century believers who, because of intense persecution, were in danger of drifting from Jesus and what God had spoken through Him. They were on a cliff edge of indecision, in jeopardy of turning away from Christianity, because the path ahead of them seemed so very, very difficult.

Why were they becoming weak? Yes, because of the great crises and trials they were enduring. But more than that, they were weak and in danger because they hadn't held to the solid moorings of God's Word. Instead of maturing and growing strong, they had regressed and made themselves weak and vulnerable.

Hebrews 5:12–14 describes what I believe to be the sad state of a great majority of those who profess Jesus.

For though by this time you ought to be teachers, you have need again for someone to teach you the elementary principles of the oracles of God, and you have come to need milk and not solid food. For everyone who partakes only of milk is not accustomed to the word of righteousness, for he is an infant. But solid food is for the mature, *who because of practice* have their senses trained to discern good and evil.

They didn't know truth for themselves. They were spiritual babies and not growing in the Word as they should. They weren't disciplining themselves, making the effort required so that they could discern truth for themselves. They had become slothful in their knowledge of God, too dependent on others, and settled for a watered-down version of the truth. (I call it "Bible lite.")

Not only had they neglected the diligent study of God's Word, but they also had neglected their fellowship with other Christians.[3] That, dear reader, is a deadly combination. When a believer turns away from the Word of God and at the same time withdraws from other believers, he or she becomes terribly vulnerable to the whispered lies of Satan, the great deceiver.

We *need* to be in gatherings of godly people. We *need* the interaction of honest, open, accountable fellowships, gatherings where iron sharpens iron.

Some of us are settling for too little in our

churches. We participate in music and worship and listen to a brief, application-oriented message, then head out the door for home.

We need *more,* don't we? We need to look deeper into the Word, studying the Bible book by book and verse by verse, and we need to grapple with important truths and doctrines. We need to do this on our own, in private study, and in the company of others who love God and love His Word.

If we don't, if we neglect His Word and His people, we will find ourselves in danger of being overwhelmed by life's bruises, setbacks, and sorrows.

THE LIFE-PRESERVING POWER OF FAITH

The victory that overcomes this world of hurt is our faith! Along with those beat-up and battered believers in the book of Hebrews, we need to fix "our eyes on Jesus, the author and perfecter of faith."

He is the One who "for the joy set before Him endured the cross, despising the shame" (12:2).

He is the One who was tested in every way we are tested.

He is the One who suffered, who succeeded in all He did, and who now sits at the right hand of the throne of God.

He is the One who lives to make intercession for you.

How I urge you, dear friend, to look to Him, fix your eyes on Him, and do not grow weary!

Toward the end of the book of Hebrews, God gives us a strong exhortation. We looked briefly at this passage earlier, but let's read it again.

For yet in a very little while, He who is coming will come, and will not delay. But My righteous one shall live by faith; and if he shrinks back, My soul has no pleasure in him. But we are not of those who shrink back to destruction, but of those who have faith to the preserving of the soul. (Hebrews 10:37–39)

It is faith, beloved, that preserves your soul, your life. All throughout this book I have sought to take you to the Word of God so that you might know and understand who God is, know and believe what He says, and then live accordingly.

Now you must decide how you are going to live when the hurt runs deep.

If you live by faith, no hurt, no matter how severe, will overcome you. Rather, you will overcome it. And even if it never goes away until you die and wake up in His presence, or until Jesus comes and catches us up to be with Him, you can live victoriously.

But in all these things we overwhelmingly conquer through Him who loved us.
Romans 8:37

HEALING TRUTHS TO REMEMBER . . . WHEN THE HURT RUNS DEEP

1. If God has allowed pain in our lives, He has allowed it for a purpose — a good purpose, because He is a good God.

2. Deep and genuine healing will always be tied to an accurate knowledge of God's sovereignty and character. The clearer our understanding of who God is, the more profound our healing will be.

3. Because God is love, and because God rules over all, everything that comes into our lives is filtered through His sovereign fingers of love.

4. Because God is all-knowing, He knows the very source of your deepest pain — and He understands exactly how to touch it, heal it, and use it to bring about your highest good.

5. No hurt is so strong that it can separate you from His love. Your hurt is not intended to drive you from God but to God.

6. Nothing that has ever happened to you has escaped God's notice. You can trust that He will bring to account everyone who has hurt you, in His time and in His way.

7. Deep hurt can happen to upright, blameless people; it is not always deserved or earned.

8. When we sin, we will find ourselves facing the consequences. But when we submit to God in repentance and seek His help, we can get through those consequences and step onto the path to hope and healing.

9. Wherever you are, whoever you are, whatever you have done, there is hope because there is God. He is a God of hope; redemption is His business.

10. God's grace is brought to fullness in our lives as we release our hurt and draw on His power in our weakness.

11. Deep, exhausting, unrelenting hurt can bring you to the end of yourself — to complete and total dependence on God — which is the best place you could ever be.

12. Whether your hurts have been caused by someone else's actions or by your own sins and failures, healing begins at the cross — the greatest expression of God's love for you.

A FINAL POSTSCRIPT

Just two more things I want to share with you, beloved.

First, after I finished writing the manuscript for *When the Hurt Runs Deep,* I had the privilege of reading two books that I believe would benefit you greatly if you are in the midst of deep hurt or know someone who is. The first is by Randy Alcorn: *If God Is Good: Faith in the Midst of Suffering and Evil.* The second, written by Les Parrott, is *You're Stronger Than You Think: The Power to Do What You Feel You Can't.* I have been so blessed by the insights of these men and would love to have referenced them earlier in this book. But I do encourage you to seek out these powerful books as you continue to grapple with God's purpose for pain.

Second, how I would love to hear from you after you read this book. I want to know if learning God's precepts on hurt and healing has made a difference. And I would so love to get you involved in one of our inductive studies of God's Word, with a group of people that will help you go even deeper. You can reach me through our Web site at www.precept.org/hurt.

INDIVIDUAL OR SMALL-GROUP STUDY GUIDE

The following questions are designed to further your journey of healing through the study of God's Word. The guide follows the structure of the book, taking you deeper into Scripture passages mentioned in each chapter with the intent that "grace and peace be multiplied to you in the knowledge of God and of Jesus our Lord" (2 Peter 1:2) as you apply God's truth to your life.

Whether you use this guide on your own, with a prayer partner, or in a small group, my fervent prayer, beloved of God, is that it will draw you more and more deeply into the Bible and into understanding God's heart for you. God longs for you to know His healing, His love, and His hope, even when the hurt runs deep.

CHAPTER ONE:
"IT WASN'T SUPPOSED TO BE THIS WAY!"

1. When in your life have you said, "It wasn't supposed to be this way"?

2. Read John 16:33. What "tribulation" is in your life right now? What would God's peace look like if you, in faith's trust, allowed it to overcome that pain?

CHAPTER TWO:
YOU DON'T SUFFER ALONE

1. Read Genesis 37:1–31. What prompted Joseph's brothers to hate him? How did their hate lead to betrayal?

2. Read Genesis 39. Why did Joseph become successful in Egypt? What did "success" look like for him in verses 1–6? In what ways was Joseph's later imprisonment also a sign of success?

3. Joseph acted with integrity yet ended up in jail. When have you suffered even when you were not to blame for something? What happened to you inside? How did you deal with it — or did you? What difference does it make today in your view of that experience to know that God was

with you every moment?

4. In what ways were Joseph's circumstances in prison similar to his circumstances in Egypt before his imprisonment?

5. Read Genesis 40. How did Joseph respond to being put in jail? What does this suggest about how God calls you to respond when you are somewhere you don't want to be?

6. What have you learned about God from the circumstances of Joseph's life so far? Stopping to assess this is so vital to your mental and spiritual health and wholeness.

CHAPTER THREE:
IS THERE PURPOSE IN YOUR PAIN?

1. Read Genesis 41:1–40. Considering the passages from Genesis that you've read in this study so far, who betrayed Joseph in his lifetime? In what ways did Joseph's response to Pharaoh (vv. 15–32) reflect humility and wisdom rather than bitterness over these betrayals? Why was he able to respond in this way? What does God want you to see?

2. Read Genesis 45:1–24. What do Joseph's

tears in front of his brothers (vv. 1–2) signify?

3. What do Joseph's words in verses 5–8 reveal about his belief in God's purposes?

4. What did Joseph tell his brothers not to do on the way home (v. 24)? Why? What does this suggest about Joseph's perspective on his suffering?

5. Read Genesis 50:20. What was Joseph placing above his emotions or pain? How did a sense of God's purpose free him to do this?

6. The psalmist recounted Joseph's story in Psalm 105. How did the psalmist begin in verses 1–4? How would you describe the perspective of these verses? Why is this significant in light of Joseph's suffering and the suffering of the Israelites? Why was Joseph's story worthy of passing down to future generations?

7. What difference does it make — in our perspective, in our ability to cope, in the lives of others — when we confront pain and find purpose in it rather than glossing over it?

CHAPTER FOUR:
WHAT KIND OF GOD ALLOWS OUR PAIN?

1. Read Psalm 103. What did the psalmist say God *does?* What words did the psalmist use to describe who God *is?*

2. How does your understanding of who *God* is affect your understanding of who *you* are? Why does your state of weakness make God's relationship with you even more significant?

3. Why is understanding the sovereignty of God important to healing?

4. Prayerfully read Revelation 21:3–5 in light of your pain today. What phrase or word brings the most hope to you? Why?

5. Why does the fact that God will one day wipe away our tears make a difference right now? What does this say about God's character and power?

6. What would you like God to "make new" (Revelation 21:5) in your life? What does God promise you about the future? Can knowing what the future holds enable you to handle the present? How? (You might

want to memorize 2 Corinthians 4:17–18 after reading the whole chapter. It's awesome!)

7. How does the truth that "God is love" (1 John 4:8) make a difference when you suffer? How does knowledge of God's love free you to find His purpose in your pain?

8. Read Romans 5:6–11. In what ways does this passage focus on realities and actions rather than emotions?

CHAPTER FIVE:
A FRIEND IN HIGH PLACES

1. Read Romans 8:28–32. What connection did Paul make between circumstances in our lives and our being conformed to Christ's image? How have you seen this happen in your own life?

2. How does God use suffering to draw us closer to Him? Describe a time when you have experienced this for yourself.

3. What characteristics of God make Him the only One who can truly heal us?

4. How does it change your view of suffering to know that *God is for you* (Romans

8:31)? What does this verse suggest about the relationship God desires with you?

5. Read Romans 8:35–39. What things do we "overwhelmingly conquer"? Who or what makes this possible? What is the number-one characteristic about God that gives us victory over pain in our lives?

CHAPTER SIX:
A TIME FOR ANGER

1. What is the difference between righteous anger and unrighteous anger?

2. Read Psalm 106:34–48. What makes God angry? Why?

3. Why is God able to be angry and love at the same time? How does His anger *demonstrate* His love for us?

4. Read Exodus 34:6–7. What difference does it make to you that God has promised to judge those who've wronged you? How does knowing this help you love others more? How does it shape your response to their behavior?

5. Read Ephesians 4:25–32. When does

anger become sinful?

6. According to this passage, what traits should replace anger and bitterness in our lives? Why? How does unresolved anger at one person affect all of our relationships?

CHAPTER SEVEN: AT THE ROOT OF YOUR PAIN

1. Read the first chapter of Job. How do Job's actions in verses 1–5 reflect what he valued the most?

2. Why did Satan suggest attacking Job? What was Satan's expectation? Why did Satan need to speak with the Lord before bringing suffering into Job's life?

3. How did Job mourn and worship God at the same time? How did his words and actions *before* his losses prepare him to respond in the way he did?

4. Read Job 2:1–10. Contrast Job's actions and words, particularly in verse 10, with what a sinful response to such suffering would look like.

5. Why did God allow pain in Job's life? How did God's interactions with Satan

reflect His love for Job?

6. Did Job get what he deserved? Why or why not? How does our culture promote the idea that your actions alone determine your future circumstances? How does this compare with what you've learned about God's sovereignty?

CHAPTER EIGHT:
LIFE CHANGES . . . GOD DOES NOT

1. Read Job 2:11–13. What is the first thing Job's friends did when they saw him? How is this similar to or different from how our culture today responds to someone's grief? When has someone responded to your suffering in a similar way?

2. What is healing about silence?

3. Read Job 3. How would you describe Job's words about his suffering? What is the difference between cursing God and Job's response to suffering? What is the difference between denying pain and Job's response?

4. Read the words of Job's friend Eliphaz in Job 5:8–27. What was Eliphaz implying about the reason for Job's suffering? What

was he suggesting about God's power to heal? Why would Eliphaz's words in verse 25 be especially cruel to Job?

5. Describe a time when someone tried to comfort you with spiritual platitudes. Were his or her words about God true or untrue? What made them hurtful to you? How did you respond to this person?

6. Thinking over what you've learned so far, what words of comfort might you offer today to someone in deep pain?

CHAPTER NINE:
GOD'S ANSWER TO OUR "WHY?"

1. When have you declared something to be true about God even though you didn't understand it?

2. Read Job 38. Who did God speak to? Describe the tone of His words. How does God's response reflect both His love and His power?

3. Read Job 40:1–5. How did Job respond to God? What did Job's words reveal about his view of God?

4. Read Job 42:1–6. What truth did Job

acknowledge about God in these verses? Why did he need to repent?

5. Why would a new appreciation for God's sovereignty comfort Job more than the words of his friends?

6. In Job 42:7, God tells Eliphaz that he is angry with him because he spoke falsely about God. Why were Job's words more acceptable to God? What does this suggest about how God wants us to relate to Him?

7. If you could choose, would you want to understand all God's ways in your life right now? Why or why not?

CHAPTER TEN:
SUFFERING WE BRING ON OURSELVES

1. Why is it tempting to blame others for our pain? What does this say about our view of ourselves?

2. Read 2 Chronicles 33:1–20. What did Manasseh do that was sinful? What do his sins have in common with all sin?

3. What caused God to respond to Manasseh and restore him to Jerusalem? Why

couldn't God heal him earlier?

4. How did God's forgiveness change Manasseh's life? Why is forgiveness powerful?

5. What are the similarities between Job's story and Manasseh's story? What are the differences? What consistencies do you see in how God responded to each man?

6. Read Psalm 51. If you did not know anything about God, what would you learn about Him from this psalm?

7. Write or pray a prayer of confession to God for any sins that you have not already confessed to Him. Your prayer doesn't need to be long or eloquent. Tell God how you have sinned. Ask Him for forgiveness. Acknowledge who you are and who He is.

8. Now, in accordance with all you have learned or know about God according to His Word, how will God respond to your prayer? Why?

9. Will you praise God for the healing that comes from knowing all is right between you and Him?

CHAPTER ELEVEN:
HAS HOPE FADED FOREVER?

1. Read Lamentations 3. How did the writer's soul respond when he dwelt on the past? What did he decide to think about instead?

2. How did remembering the characteristics of God restore hope to the writer of Lamentations? Why would Satan want him to dwell instead on circumstances?

3. What do the writer's words suggest about how he viewed God? In what ways did his knowledge of God shape his response to suffering?

4. What changes over time in this passage, and what stays the same?

5. Why is it hopeful to dwell on who God is rather than on your past actions?

6. How might the story of your life point others to hope in God?

Chapter Twelve:
Walking Through the Fire . . .
but Not Alone!

1. Read Daniel 3. When have you faced persecution — in your family, workplace, or community — because of your faith in God?

2. Why were Shadrach, Meshach, and Abednego able to say they did not need to defend themselves against Nebuchadnezzar? How do you tend to react to those who unjustly cause you pain or subject you to persecution? What does your natural response reveal about your view of God? your view of suffering?

3. What does Shadrach, Meshach, and Abednego's reaction to Nebuchadnezzar say about who they believed God to be? What do their words reveal about their priorities, about what mattered most to them?

4. Who was the fourth man in the furnace? Why was he there? How does God's presence make a difference even when we are experiencing pain?

5. What would it look like in your life to

trust God even when you don't know if He will rescue you from pain? What do you need to believe about God's nature — as opposed to human nature — in order to trust Him?

6. How might your response to difficult times lead others to God?

CHAPTER THIRTEEN: THE LINGERING HURT OF SUICIDE

1. What are the greatest or most troubling issues you have to deal with when you think of a loved one, or anyone, who committed suicide? What have you learned in this chapter that has helped you with those questions? What issues are not covered that you would like to discuss? (I, Kay, would love to know so I could be of more help. You can reach me through our Web site at www.precept.org/hurt.)

2. Do you find yourself worrying about where the person who committed suicide is? What have you learned from the scriptures in this chapter that can help you handle this worry?

3. Read Philippians 4:8–9. What does God call you to think about right now? Make a

list of these eight descriptive phrases. Take each memory or question you have about your loved one's suicide (or other circumstances leading to the pain you are in) and compare it to the list you just made. If it does not match God's criteria for your thoughts, what will you do about it?

4. Is it disobedient to dwell on the past in destructive ways? Why or why not?

5. Read Philippians 3:13–14. What would it look like to "forget" what lies behind in your life? Do you believe it's possible to truly "forget"? Why or why not? What would it look like for you to reach forward to "what lies ahead"?

6. Ask God to show you how these verses can bring healing from your loved one's suicide or your suicidal thoughts. Express your anger and your pain to Him. Ask Him to guide your thoughts to the traits of Philippians 4:8–9 and pray those traits out loud. Although healing can be slow, keep returning to God with your pain and your desire to submit your mind and heart to Him.

Chapter Fourteen:
Pulling the Plug on Pain

1. When have you had to sacrifice something that was precious to you? How did that experience change you?

2. Read Genesis 22:1–19. How did Abraham's willingness to let go of Isaac make room for God to reveal Himself? In what way was Abraham's obedience an act of worship?

3. How did Abraham's obedience foreshadow Jesus' obedience in the Garden of Gethsemane (Luke 22:42)? What did God do for Abraham that He did not do for Jesus? Why?

4. Read 2 Corinthians 12:7–10. Why did Paul have a "thorn in the flesh"? How was God glorified through this thorn? What connection did Paul make between letting go of his human desire and drawing closer to God?

5. What pain do you need to pull the plug on, to let go of — with total confidence that what you are doing is biblical? And what would change for you if you did? Why haven't you done so? Do you want

to be well?

CHAPTER FIFTEEN:
THE BENEFITS OF SUFFERING

1. Read Matthew 13:1–9, 18–23. Has suffering ever caused you to turn away from God? If so, when?

2. What emotional or physical scars do you have as a result of living in this crooked and perverse generation? In what ways can these scars give you hope for heaven?

3. What would it look like for God to redeem the pain you are in right now?

4. Read Philippians 3:7–11. What words did Paul use to describe earthly accomplishments and things? Why? List all the words in this passage that Paul used to reflect his deepest desires. What was his ultimate goal?

5. Read 2 Corinthians 4:16–18. What does the "outer man" represent? What does the "inner man" represent? What does your outer self look like right now? How does it compare to your inner self?

6. What does affliction lead to, according to

verse 17?

7. What things do you "see" in your pain today (verse 18)? What things are happening through your pain that you cannot see? Which will last for eternity?

CHAPTER SIXTEEN:
THE HURT YET TO COME

1. When have you experienced pain or persecution because of your religious beliefs? Did the pain surprise you? Why or why not?

2. Read 1 Peter 2:19–25. For what purpose has God called you? How do you know?

3. How did Christ respond to suffering? What purpose did His suffering have? What does this say about the value of our suffering as Christ followers?

4. Read 1 Peter 3:14–18. What did Paul instruct us to do when we suffer for God's glory? What are we *not* to do?

5. How can you tell if your suffering is because of righteousness or because of sin? Why does it make a difference?

6. Read 1 Peter 5:10. What does God promise to do for you? Why does He want you to know this promise?

CHAPTER SEVENTEEN:
HOW CAN JESUS POSSIBLY UNDERSTAND YOUR PAIN?

1. Read Matthew 26:36–46. Describe a time when your soul was "deeply grieved." Did you go to a particular place to pray or cry?

2. What did Jesus ask His friends to do? Why? How did Jesus respond when He found His friends sleeping?

3. Have you ever asked a friend to be with you when you were grieving or waiting for difficult news? What happened? Why does loneliness so often accompany grief?

4. How many times did Jesus pray the same prayer? What is the "cup" He referred to? What do His prayers suggest about His relationship with His Father?

5. Which aspect of Jesus' suffering did you identify with the most? Why?

6. What difference does it make in your perspective on pain to know that Jesus

understands your suffering because He, too, suffered?

7. Think over everything you learned in this chapter. How will you respond to the Father and the Son in light of these truths? Write out or pour out in prayer the words on your heart.

CHAPTER EIGHTEEN:
WILL THE HURT EVER GO AWAY?

1. Read Hebrews 10:11–23. What did the priests do again and again? What was the result? What have you done or said over and over to try to redeem pain in your life? How well did that work?

2. How many sacrifices did Jesus make (vv. 12–13)? For how long? How does Jesus' sacrifice influence you? What does this imply about *your* ability to redeem your pain?

3. The Holy Spirit testifies that Jesus' sacrifice is a sign of God's covenant (v. 16). What does God do to seal this covenant with us?

4. Why can we draw near to God with confidence? How does this confidence

lead to hope?

5. Read Ephesians 4:31–5:2. What does bitterness lead to? Why?

6. Why does God call us to forgive others? How does our forgiveness of others remind us of God's forgiveness of us? Does God expect us to forgive others out of our own power? Why or why not?

7. When have you seen the inability to forgive cause someone greater pain? In what way does forgiveness loosen the grip of the past on our lives?

CONCLUSION: LIFE-PRESERVING WORDS

1. Read Romans 5:1–5. What are we called to exult in? What result does tribulation ultimately bring?

2. When has disappointment caused you to dwell in pain rather than risking hope?

3. According to this passage, what kind of hope does God give? Why? How might a confidence in God's hope free you to have joy again — to exult?

4. Throughout this study, we have looked at passages that contrast dwelling on the past with hoping in the future. Why does hoping in the future make such a difference in our healing? What do we learn from the fact that God speaks words of hope so often in Scripture?

5. What practical changes could you make (such as meeting more regularly with a community of believers, getting more sleep, memorizing Scripture) that would further God's work of healing in your life?

6. Looking back on the twelve healing truths outlined in this book (see pages 359–61 for the full list), which ones resonate with you the most right now? What could you do to remember these truths when you need them most?

APPENDIX:
A FEW PRACTICAL HELPS

How do you get through the day (and the night that follows) when the hurt runs so terribly deep?

It's such a very real question for those who are reeling from personal pain. You need to have ready a practical plan of action, so you don't have to figure it all out when it's hard to think or you're just plain worn out. So let me number a few timely reminders for you. Perhaps they could be part of a checklist that you post in some highly visible place or use as a bookmark in your Bible.

1. Make sure you consciously inject, include, acknowledge God in every situation.

When Paul wrote the believers in Thessalonica who were suffering greatly because of the gospel, he urged them to rejoice always, pray without ceasing, and give thanks in everything.[1]

What was he doing? He was urging them to stay in constant communication with God and to walk in faith. This is how I believe you "inject" God into every situation; He's the medicine, the strength you need to keep on functioning! The healing for your hurt is found in your total, moment-by-moment dependence on God until leaning on Him becomes your habit. In Philippians 4:13 Paul wrote, "I can do all things through Him who strengthens me." Another way to translate that is "through Him who constantly infuses [present tense] His strength in me."

In Psalm 69, King David wrote of the waters that had threatened his life, the deep mire he was in, and those who hated him. He wrote of his tears, weeping, the reproach of others, and his distress. And then in verses 29 and 30 he said, "But I am afflicted and in pain; may Your salvation, O God, set me securely on high. I will praise the name of God with song and magnify Him with thanksgiving."

What was David doing? *He was bringing God into the situation.* This is what it means to pray without ceasing. To put it into a contemporary setting, it's like texting God, talking with Him about everything. Constant communication! Talking over everything with Him demonstrates your dependence on God and your need for Him. It connects you with Him "who is able to do far more abundantly beyond all that we ask or think." It takes you beyond yourself and turns on "the power that works within us" (Ephesians 3:20).

This triad — *rejoicing always, praying without ceasing,* and *giving thanks always for all things* — is a declaration of faith and trust that not only pleases God, but strengthens you, giving you a divine energy that enables you to continue. The very act of doing all this reminds you that God is there for you and you are not alone. Listen to what David wrote in Psalm 22:3–5.

Yet You are holy,
   O You who are enthroned upon the praises of Israel.
In You our fathers trusted;
   They trusted and You delivered them.
To You they cried out and were delivered;
   In You they trusted and were not disappointed.

One of my "precious faces" on Facebook e-mailed me and asked,

When one has experienced significant trauma . . . particularly childhood trauma, is it possible or likely that this person could or would experience complete emotional healing? I know the textbook answer — "All things are possible with God" — but I would like to dissect this issue a bit deeper.

She noted that many people who have surrendered their lives to God still endure the pain and fears that accompany traumatic experiences.

I believe that God can and does work through therapists, physicians, and medication, but what if one chooses not to go that route and simply trust God for emotional healing?

Is emotional healing like physical healing . . . sometimes God chooses to heal by restoring health and sometimes He allows the person to die? Is this the same with emotional healing . . . sometimes God chooses to heal by "fixing" the damaged heart, brain, thought processes, etc., and sometimes He allows the "emotional handicap" to continue?

Another author wrote that optimism, love, and courage are qualities that propel us past pain.[2] Stop and think of that statement, in light of what you've read of God's Word in this book, the truths He wants us to know and live by.

Yes, if I had a brain injury, I would certainly want to take advantage of all science has learned. As to emotional healing, however, I would answer my Facebook friend in this way: because of all I've read in the Word of God, I truly believe emotional healing is possible. Further, I believe that rejoicing always, praying without ceasing, and giving thanks always is part of that healing.

2. Find what lifts your spirits.

Sometimes it helps to express yourself by writing in a journal, pouring out your heart to God on paper, translating your thoughts into words that you can read again and mull over in your mind. (Isn't this essentially what we see David doing in the book of Psalms?)

Or you may pour out your heart through poetry or through songs in the night when sleep eludes you. Sometimes it helps just to get it out — to express it in some way so that it's off your mind and you can rest. If it helps to lift the burden, to get it off your heart into a journal or poured out in another creative way, do it. If it doesn't help, then don't continue. Simple as that.

I've tried my hand at journaling from time to time, but that's not what helps me most. My greatest help and comfort comes from quietly bathing myself in God's Word. Reading and letting it wash over my soul. That's when I realize that nothing is important but God and His pleasure, not mine. He is the sovereign, and I bow in trust. Eventually, of course, those biblical precepts reemerge in my teaching and writing.

Another thing I like to do is read the biographies of other Christians, especially those from days gone by, and watch how they dealt with suffering, rejection, betrayal, persecution, and hurt that runs deep. Observing their lives, I am encouraged to persevere, to be His valiant one.

3. Make sure you give your body what it needs.

Hurt takes its toll physically. I remember when I was with my mother in Florida, and the hospital called in the middle of the night to tell us that my dad's heart had stopped but they got it going again. They thought we might want to come to the hospital as soon as possible.

I fell to my knees, because I thought God had told me my father would live and that he would survive the three surgeries he'd had in five days. But now it seemed as if he might not live after all.

What worried me most was that I wasn't sure my father was truly saved. He had been a minister, yes, but there had been no true spiritual understanding and fellowship between us since I received Christ at age twenty-nine. As I began crying out to God, my heart wouldn't stop pounding in my chest. I wanted it to be quiet. I wanted my body to be still, but it just wouldn't co-operate.

Hurt, stress, and anxiety all affect us physically, whether we want to acknowledge it or not. This is why we need to take particularly good care of our bodies in difficult times. Rest, proper nutrition, adequate light, and exercise are important to our health and restorative to mind, body, and spirit. It's hard to think clearly and objectively or keep it together emotionally when you are tired, when your body hasn't been receiving the nutrients it needs, or when you stagnate in the house and shut out the light.

I could elaborate for pages here, but please just take my counsel that you need to be at your physical best when the hurt runs deep. Force yourself to eat correctly and regularly, even if you can only take small bites at a time. When your blood sugar goes down, *you* go down. Eat as many natural foods as you can, and watch your intake of processed sugar.

Learn about the importance of a good night's sleep, and how to get it. *Then do it.* I used to think it wasn't spiritual to sleep. I later learned that my body was crying out for it and that I was damaging myself by continually denying my need for rest. Over time, however, God showed me it was presumptuous sin if I thought I could break His natural laws and get away with it.

When my son was so ill, when my daughter-in-law died, and when other difficult things came into our lives and getting a night's sleep became so terribly difficult, I used a sleeping pill for several nights — and I didn't set my alarm. I gave myself permission to sleep. As far as I'm concerned, the darker the room, the better. Because my husband often gets up in the night and needs to keep on a light, I wear soft eyeshades.

If you find it hard to rest, here's a solution that works for many. Make a cup of decaffeinated tea (chamomile tea is a soothing bedtime beverage). Sip it in a quiet atmosphere, with the lights turned down low, and then head for bed.

If the life of the body is in the blood, as the Word of God says, then you have to get that oxygenated blood to the cells. Exercise gets it there — even if it's simply getting up and walking around the house.

And may I say just one word about light? Your body needs it, as do your soul and spirit! It triggers what your body needs to lift its moods and secrete the chemicals you need. Sunshine is important. Make a point of getting outside in the sun for at least twenty minutes a day. Bask in the light, and remember that Jesus is the Light of life.[3]

4. Resist the tendency to isolate yourself.

When we're hurting, our tendency may be to close ourselves off from others. This is one of the signs of depression, and you can't stay there and get well. Proverbs 17:17 says, "A friend loves at all times, and a brother is born for adversity." We need the *right* people to come alongside us. So don't pull the curtains, lock the door, or refuse to answer your phone.

Don't isolate yourself, no matter how you feel. If you think no one wants to be with you, if you're worried about bringing others low, or if you've bought into the lie that you're not worthy of being with, remember that God put us into a body — His body, the church. Part of our calling as a church is to minister to others, to "bear one another's burdens, and thereby fulfill the law of Christ" (Galatians 6:2).

Ecclesiastes 4:9–12 says,

> Two are better than one because they have a good return for their labor. For if either of them falls, the one will lift up his companion. But woe to the one who falls when there is not another to lift him up. Furthermore, if two lie down together they keep warm, but how can one be warm alone? And if one can overpower him who is alone, two can resist him. A cord of three strands is not quickly torn apart.

To which you may reply, "But no one has shown up!"

Then pray. Ask God to send someone to you. Not as a substitute for God, but as a friend or a wise counselor. Then wait for God's answer. He may lead you to call the church and tell the pastor or a staff member your situation. But let me caution you: make sure it's a church that believes the Bible is the Word of God and holds the answer to every situation and circumstance of life. Ask them if they know someone who is godly, mature, and well-grounded in the Word of God who would be willing to talk with you, to listen, and to pray.

Just make sure, though, that you really want to get well.

Don't be offended by my statement; I got it from Jesus.[4] Sometimes when we have suffered rejection, we have a tendency to think all sorts of crazy and unbiblical thoughts. We may even get so far off-track that we drive people away by putting them in the position only God should hold. Or we become bitter and don't respond to people properly. We suspect they have ulterior motives for offering help, or we accuse them of being like all the rest who eventually walk out!

If this is where you are, don't seek out anyone yet. Instead, go back and read through this book again, searching out the scriptures I've shared, before you call for help.

The fact is, some people *want* to stay where they are because it becomes their excuse for not changing. They have become so used to playing the blame game that they don't know any other way to respond. Others stay where they are because they think this is the only way they can get the attention they want.

But that sort of attention doesn't last, and it's not what our hearts truly long for.

Think about it, beloved. Ask God about what I am saying.

5. Master your thoughts, or your thoughts will master you.

Your greatest enemy can be thoughts of your past. You must not allow the hurt of the past to determine your future in any way but for good. Remember, God will redeem your past in order to achieve His purpose. Evil or hurtful as it may have been, it can still be used for your good if you will believe God.

You must learn to think biblically, to bring every thought captive to the obedience of Jesus Christ, as 2 Corinthians 10:5 tells us. Bring each thought up against the plumb line of God's Word to make sure it's straight and true.

Don't live in a past you cannot change. *What ifs* and *if onlys* are smoke and vapor, not reality. They will only increase your misery.

"But," you say, "the thought won't go away."

Remember, beloved, you are in warfare, and your enemy, the devil, wants you to think the way he directs. He is the master of lies and deception, so beware! If you are a child of God, however, you have the mind of Christ.[5] So every time the devil raps at the door of your mind with his lies, deceptions, and tormenting thoughts, don't open the door and invite him in! Refuse to answer his knock. Pray, sing, or meditate on Scripture — activities that meet all the qualifications of Philippians 4:8. Eventually Satan will tire and depart.

How well I know. I've had my own share of such warfare. Don't forget that the battle is for your mind, which is the command center of life. Master your thoughts with truth, and you will master your mental well-being. "For as he thinks within himself, so he is" (Proverbs 23:7).

6. Read the Psalms.

I have a friend who lost his wife after twenty-five years of marriage, and he told me that for months his Bible became about a quarter-inch thick. Why? Because he just camped in the book of Psalms. He read and read and read Psalms, day and night. He went to bed with them, got up with them, and went back to them again and again through the day.

Whatever brokenness you may have experienced in your life, the Psalms will penetrate to your deepest hurt. If you can't sleep at night, read them out loud, and then talk to God about what you read. Speak to Him audibly, just as you would your best friend. Pour out your soul to Him. Get a pencil and write your thoughts, your prayers, your questions in the margins of your Bible, next to verses that grab your heart. Put a date beside it and then come back and read it later . . . and rejoice over how far God has brought you.

7. Play music, sing, and (if you can) laugh.

Listen to music that soothes or lifts your spirit.

Sing, even if you don't want to, even if it brings tears to your eyes. Force yourself to sing. As Solomon tells us, "A joyful heart is good medicine" (Proverbs 17:22).

Watch programs or movies that are edifying and enriching, not disturbing or stressful.

And laugh, my friend.

Yes, you read me right.

It's all right to laugh even when the hurt runs deep. It is healthy, as it releases God-created feel-good chemicals into your body.

And speaking of God's chemicals, last but

not least, touch is healing. The skin is the largest sense organ in the body with more than five million receptors. Is it any wonder, then, that researchers have found that safe, caring touches are good for the mind, body, and spirit of an individual? Touch, they have found, reduces stress, boosts immunity, lessens the blues, and eases pain as it stimulates the brain to produce endorphins (the body's natural analgesics).

A pat, a rubbing of the shoulders, a hug, a "holy kiss,"[6] or a massage can all help, especially when the hurt runs deep.

NOTES

Chapter 1

1. Mark Seal and Eleanor Squillari, "Hello, Madoff!" The Madoff Chronicles, Part II: What the Secretary Saw, *Vanity Fair,* June 2009, 162.

Chapter 4

1. Jeremiah 31:3.

Chapter 5

1. Genesis 3:15.
2. Genesis 16:13.
3. 2 Thessalonians 1:8.

Chapter 6

1. Exodus 22:22–24; Deuteronomy 29:18–21; Jeremiah 25:6; Psalm 106:34–40; Deuteronomy 4:23–26.
2. Jeremiah 25:6–11.
3. Joshua 7:1; Numbers 11:1, 33; 12:1–9.
4. Psalm 78:21–22; Hebrews 3:7–12; John

3:36; Romans 1:18.
5. Romans 1:20–24.
6. Psalm 2:10–12.
7. Zechariah 2:8–9.
8. Romans 2:5.
9. John 8:28–29.
10. Isaiah 45:21.
11. Genesis 49:6–7; 1 Samuel 25:26, 31.
12. Job 36:13.
13. Hosea 7:6.
14. Proverbs 29:22, 30:33.
15. Proverbs 27:4.
16. Psalm 55:3; 1 Samuel 17:28.
17. Proverbs 29:22.
18. Proverbs 22:24–25.
19. Hebrews 12:15.

Chapter 7
1. Revelation 12:9; 20:2.

Chapter 9
1. Revelation 4:11.
2. Job 33:13.

Chapter 10
1. Isaiah 61:3, KJV.
2. Genesis 15:7–21, 13:14–17.
3. 2 Kings 21.

Chapter 11

1. J. Gerald Harris, "Atlanta: a center of sexual exploitation?" *The Christian Index,* July 30, 2009, http://christianindex.org/5678.article.
2. Lamentations 1:7.
3. James 1:15.
4. Lamentations 2:14.
5. This is the message of Romans 3:21–5:21.
6. 1 Kings 21:27–29.
7. 2 Corinthians 10:5.

Chapter 12

1. Hebrews 13:8.
2. Psalm 23:4.
3. Hebrews 3:1–6.

Chapter 13

1. Deuteronomy 32:39; Psalm 139:16.
2. James 3:5–6.
3. "In everything give thanks; for this is God's will for you in Christ Jesus" (1 Thessalonians 5:18).
4. "And we know that God causes all things to work together for good to those who love God, to those who are called according to His purpose. For those whom He foreknew, He also predestined to become conformed to the image of His Son, so

that He would be the firstborn among many brethren; and these whom He predestined, He also called; and these whom He called, He also justified; and these whom He justified, He also glorified" (Romans 8:28–30).

5. 2 Corinthians 5:6.
6. Revelation 20:14–15; Isaiah 66:22–24; Mark 9:48.
7. Psalm 107:20.

Chapter 14

1. Genesis 12.
2. 1 Corinthians 15:28.
3. Hebrews 11:19.
4. Nancy Guthrie, *Hearing Jesus Speak into Your Sorrow* (Carol Stream, IL: Tyndale, 2009), xiii–xiv.
5. Jeremiah 1:12.
6. Ephesians 5:20.
7. I have written a Precept Upon Precept course that God has used powerfully in the lives of single and married people over the years. Titled "Marriage Without Regrets," the course takes the student to the Word of God for His precepts for life on every aspect of marriage, including divorce and remarriage. For more information, visit our website: www.precept.org.
8. I'm in the company of godly male teach-

ers such as John MacArthur and Chuck Swindoll, just to name two.
9. John 8:36.

Chapter 15

1. Matthew 13:10–35.
2. Hebrews 5:8.
3. Deuteronomy 32:51.
4. Psalm 51:4.
5. 2 Samuel 24:10–25.
6. Acts 13:22.
7. Psalm 56:8.
8. Job 3.
9. 1 Kings 19:4.
10. Jeremiah 20:14–18.
11. 2 Corinthians 5:1–8.
12. Philippians 1:23.
13. Galatians 6:17.
14. Romans 11:25–29.
15. Exodus 6:30.
16. Isaiah 14:27.
17. 2 Corinthians 12:1–9.
18. Sharon was referring to a series of devotional Bible studies I've written that God has used in surprising and significant ways. They introduce the reader or small group to the skills of inductive study and, in the process, help you see truth for yourself. A listing of these studies is in the back of this book. For information on ad-

ditional studies available through Precept Ministries International, go to www.precept.org or call 1-800-763-8280.
19. Hebrews 12:25–29.
20. Matthew 10:38–39.

Chapter 16
1. John 14:27, 16:33; Romans 5:1, 8:6, 28.
2. Philippians 3:10.
3. John 7:3.
4. Mark 3:21.
5. John F. Walvoord and Roy B. Zuck, *The Bible Knowledge Commentary: An Exposition of the Scriptures,* vol. 2 (Wheaton, IL: Victor, 1983), 848.
6. Proverbs 18:21.
7. Ephesians 6:13.
8. Hebrews 13:5–6.

Chapter 17
1. John 6:70.
2. Isaiah 50:6.
3. Hebrews 12:2.
4. 2 Corinthians 5:21.
5. Hebrews 10:12.

Chapter 18
1. Nancy Sharman, *Creating a Legacy of Joy* (Reva, VA: Victory Publishing, 2008), 22.
2. Sharman, *Legacy of Joy,* 26.

3. Nancy Sharman's story is written in the little booklet *Creating a Legacy of Joy.* It's a wonderful witness to have with you to share with those whose hurt runs deep. Nancy is now a pastor, Christian counselor, court-certified educator, gifted teacher, and women's conference speaker. A precious woman who has allowed me the privilege of sharing her story of redemption with you.
4. Sharman, *Legacy of Joy,* 36.
5. If you don't know how to read the Bible in such a way that you can understand it, that is why God raised up Precept Ministries International. This is what we are all about, and we are all about it in 150 countries and 70 languages! You can find us at www.precept.org.
6. Hebrews 2:14.
7. Ephesians 1:13–14.
8. Kay Arthur, David Lawson, and BJ Lawson, *Forgiveness: Breaking the Power of the Past* (Colorado Springs: WaterBrook, 2007), 32.
9. Genesis 18:25.

Conclusion
1. Romans 4:4–5:5.
2. J. Strong, *The exhaustive concordance of the Bible: Showing every word of the text of*

the common English version of the canonical books, and every occurrence of each word in regular order. (electronic ed.) (Ontario: Woodside Bible Fellowship, 1996), G5281.

3. Hebrews 10:25.

Appendix

1. 1 Thessalonians 5:16–18.
2. Dan Baker, *What Happy People Know* (New York: Rodale, 2003), 18.
3. John 1:4.
4. John 5:6.
5. 1 Corinthians 2:12–16.
6. Romans 16:16; 1 Corinthians 16:20; 2 Corinthians 13:12; 1 Thessalonians 5:26.

ACKNOWLEDGMENTS

God saves us and puts us in a body because no one individual can do it all . . . and whatever is done is to be done for the edification of His church and for the glory of the One who is the head of the body, our Lord Jesus Christ. To Him alone belongs glory, honor, and power. Therefore, whatever comes of this labor of love for the body of Christ is because of God's grace in allowing me to work with two godly, patient, loving souls:

Larry Libby, who, although an excellent writer in his own right, humbly serves as a kind and gentle editor par excellence, making my rough places smooth, and . . .

Laura Barker, who reads the manuscript for you, the reader, and makes sure the material flows and the message is complete — and does it was such grace and encouragement.

Thank you, dear ones. I am so much better because of you than I would be alone.

ABOUT KAY ARTHUR AND PRECEPT MINISTRIES INTERNATIONAL

Kay Arthur is known around the world as an international Bible teacher, author, conference speaker, and host of the national radio and television programs *Precepts for Life,* which reach a worldwide viewing audience of over 94 million. A four-time Gold Medallion Award–winning author, Kay has authored more than 100 books and Bible studies.

Kay and her husband, Jack, founded Precept Ministries International in 1970 in Chattanooga, Tennessee, with a vision to establish people in God's Word. Today, the ministry has a worldwide outreach. In addition to inductive study training workshops and thousands of small-group studies across America, PMI reaches nearly 150 countries with inductive Bible studies translated into nearly 70 languages, teaching people to discover Truth for themselves.

Contact Precept Ministries International

for more information:
Precept Ministries International
PO Box 182218
Chattanooga, TN 37422-7218
800-763-8280
www.precept.org